"*This book was written by a self made hard working entrepreneur, Matt Shoup. If you want to discover specific steps to building your award winning business – stop looking. This book will give you great insight to an often difficult process of making your customers "spread the word" about your product or business!*"

Ken McElroy, CEO of MC Companies & Author of *The ABC's of Real Estate Investing, The Sleeping Giant, Rich Dad's Advisors: The ABC's of Property Management, The Advanced Guide to Real Estate Investing, Rich Dad's Advisors: The Advanced Guide to Real Estate Investing, Rich Dad's: The ABC's of Real Estate Investing*

"*From first glance to in-depth study, Matt Shoup and his new book offer comfortable insight and hard-driving results—you can feel the enthusiasm jump off the page.*"

Rick Griggs, Founder, Quid Novi Innovation Festival

"*Become an Award Winning Company is a must-read for every entrepreneur. Reading this book and hearing Matt speak live on this topic has inspired and motivated me to pay attention to this realm of business. Matt's book goes straight to the point and shows any entrepreneur in any industry how to win awards and leverage them for success. This $25 investment will add tens of thousands of dollars to my bottom line!*

Rachael Jayne Groover, Founder, The YIN Project

"*This book is a lot like its author- full of energy and specific ideas to help you and your company reach Rockstar status.*"

Eric Thompson, President, The Group, Inc. Real Estate

If you're able, scan this with your mobile device before you read this book.

The author is available for speaking engagements, seminars and other
multimedia presentations.

Published by:
Shoup Consulting, LLC
540 W. 66th St B1
Loveland, CO 80538

www.BecomeAnAwardWinningCompany.com
www.BAAWC.com
www.MattShoup.com

Photos courtesy of Thomas J. Waido,
www.waidopro.com

Cover, graphics and interior layout designed by Bold Frog Design, LLC.
www.boldfrogdesign.com

Printed in the United States of America

Become an Award Winning Company
Matt Shoup
1. Title 2. Author 3. Commerce: Business

HF5001-6182	...........Business
HF5387-5387.5	...........Business ethics
HF5410-5417.5	...........Marketing. Distribution of products
HF5801-6182	...........Advertising

ISBN-10: 0983811709
ISBN-13: 978-0983811701

BECOME AN AWARD WINNING COMPANY

7 Simple Steps to Unlock the Million Dollar Secret Every Entrepreneur Needs to Know

MATT SHOUP

SHOUP CONSULTING ©2012

Emily, Riley, and Hailey, I love you three with all my heart.
This book is dedicated to you.

ACKNOWLEDGMENTS

My dream to become an author has been realized, and I could not have done it without the help, support, love, and encouragement I received from the following people:

First and all thanks go to Jesus. I give you all the credit. Thank you for the gifts you have given me, for your sacrifice for the world, and for leading me and my life.

To my beautiful wife, Emily, thank you so much for all your love, support, and encouragement. Thanks for putting up with all my craziness, and the long hours and days I spent on this book. And, before the final trip to get it done, I will never forget that extra 20 minutes you spent at DIA, and the conversation we had; it was perfect timing. You are my best friend, and I am proud to call you my wife and the mother of our children. Thank you for always being there for me, and for your input on this book. I could not have done this without you. I love you with all my heart!

Riley and Hailey, you two are my little angels, and I love you. Thank you for all the love you bring to Daddy's life. I am proud of you both and proud to be your dad. Can't wait for you to read Dadda's book!

My parents, Paul and Nancy: I love you both. Thank you for teaching me from a young age to work hard for what I want in life, and for never giving me a handout. Thanks for letting me start my first small businesses, and supporting me through the one that almost got me kicked out of school.

Steve and Carrie Earll, thank you for inspiring me and encouraging me to write, for your input, support, and prayers, and for being there for me over the years. It is an honor to be your daughter's husband.

Dave Sward, thank you, "tio," for all your support and input for this book, as well as your friendship over the years. Thanks for always being there when I was making tough decisions, and for telling it like it was when I needed to be told. I will never forget, in the months before this book release, when you dropped everything you were doing to stop by for that margarita! You are one of the few people I would run next to with the bulls in Spain (or sit on the fence with and watch). Next time we order a whole cochinillo.

A big shout out to Entrepreneurs' Organization (EO). I have received so much value from EO over the years, and I appreciate all the connections and friendships I have made within the organization.

Fight Club Forum (David McLain, Tom Prudence, Nathan Mendel, Alicia Chong, and Russell Lundstrom), thank you for all of your input, suggestions, and help with the book. I couldn't have done this without you. I love you all.

A huge shout out to the entire M & E Painting team and family. How could I talk about becoming an award-winning company if I didn't have an award-winning team? You guys and gals are all amazing. Thank you for the loyalty, dedication, and effort you put into the company every day. With this team, I know I can look forward to winning many more awards in the years to come.

Braun Mincher, thanks for your friendship and support over the years. I also appreciate your help, input, and ideas with this book. You are a rockstar!

Pepita y Miguel, mi familia española; Gracias por abrir las puertas de vuestra casa, a mí y mi familia, y por mostrarnos el amor de la gente de España. Estaré agradecido por siempre. Y no os preocupéis, aun con el éxito que está por venir y todo que pase, siempre seré el Mateo que conocisteis por primera vez. ¡Hasta pronto!

Ryan Spencer, thanks for always being there for me, and for holding me accountable. It is an honor to be your friend.

Kira Berberich, thank you for all of the hard work you have done on this book. You are the behind-the-scenes hero who helped to make it happen.

Melissa Marsh and Bold Frog Design: WOW! This book cover, design, and layout look awesome! Thanks for taking my dream and vision for this book and designing it into a masterpiece. Also, thanks for your suggestions along the way. You are amazing at what you do.

Cindi Lods, I always feel gratitude to you and your family for giving me a chance as I was first starting my business. I will never forget my first customer. You helped me to become an award-winning company and write this book. (Told you I would do it!)

Rick Griggs, what a pleasure to know you. Every time I talk to you, I learn something new. You have truly inspired me, and it is an honor to learn from you.

Amy Madden Copp, thank you for all your help, planning, and input into the book release and launch party. It has been an honor to know you.

Ken McElroy, thank you for your inspiration, time, and pushing me to write this book sooner than I had planned (not sure if you knew you did that, but you did).

Dave Ramsey, thank you for all you and The Lampo Group have taught me over the years, both personally and professionally. I am honored to know you and honored that you helped me make this book a success.

Sergio Carbajo Garcia, my friend from the other side of the globe, thank you for your friendship, support, and a point of view that always seems to contrast mine. It is has been a pleasure to spend time with you, and have you be there for me as a friend (and translator). Looking forward to the castellano version of this book.

Terry Cleland (Skippy), it has been an honor to know you over the past decade. I would never be where I am today in business if it wasn't for you teaching me so much, setting an example, and being part of the M & E team.

Renae Weidenkeller, thank you for jumping right in at one of the most crucial times in my business to help me make this book, and all other ventures a success. Looking forward to many more years to come.

Karen Marcus, a big thank you for your help, support, input, and availability during the last weeks before this book's release. I couldn't have done it without you.

Cristina Blanco, gracias por ser una gran amiga y por el apoyo y amistad sobre esta última década. ¡Agradezco tus consejos sobre esta publicación y su éxito en España!

Sandra Pike, thank you for all of your hard work leading up to the release of this book. I couldn't have done this without you. Don't stop til you reach that dream.

Tom Toomer, thank you for your years of friendship, mentoring, and support. Your timing of coming back into my life was impeccable.

Matt Landauer, thank you for teaching me so much about business over the years. I will never forget payroll Friday on the 16th Street Mall.

Andrea Costantine, thank you for sitting down with me and taking me through the steps and procedures to make this book happen.

Jeff Winchester, thank you for your friendship over the years and for being my first official cool boss. Always have to thank you again for the window.

Amanda Ericson, thanks for always pushing Shoopy to be the top 1% of Matts that you know. It has been an honor to know you and have you as my friend.

Uncle Terry, thank you for sharing all of your business experience, insight and knowledge over the years.

Bon and Jim Fillpot, thanks for throwing that computer in my lap.

To all of the award-winning CEOs that I interviewed for this book, thank you all for taking the time to share with me how you became a Become an Award Winning Company (BAAWC) Rockstar! This book could not have been possible without you all.

Ruth Rennie, as I wrote this book, I realized you were one of the only teachers I had growing up who realized my potential and worked with me to reach it. So, thank you. I have valued staying in touch with you.

Chris Suria (aka Capn' Cannoli) an honor to know you and to have your friendship for 25 years and counting.

Mamen y Javi, ha sido un honor conoceros y teneros en nuestra vida. Nunca nos olvidaremos de nuestras aventuras americanas y viajes juntos. Haciendo kilómetros con descapotables, aviones por todos lados, porquerías para comer, los mejores monumentos de los EEUU, pistoleros, barbacoas, Levi's, fútbol americano, desayunos con vista a las montañas, tejas volando por todos lados, inundaciones a rebasar, y lo mejor de todo: teneros, nuestra familia, con nosotros.

If I am forgetting anybody, I apologize; I owe you a copy of this book!

TABLE OF CONTENTS

PART III: *More Benefits*

PART IV: *The 7 Simple Steps and Other Tips for Becoming an Award Winning Company*

◊ **Chapter 18.** Award Winning Myths Set Straight 147

◊ **Chapter 19.** The 7 Simple Steps 155

◊ **Chapter 20.** Tips for the BAAWC Rockstar 171

◊ **Chapter 21.** Conclusion 181

Appendix I: Matt's Companies 183

Appendix II: Resources 189

PART I:

My Story, Your Story, and the Million Dollar Secret Every Entrepreneur Needs to Know

CHAPTER 1

Introduction

So Why Read This Book?

$100,000 or your money back, that's why!

Imagine finishing this book and being able to immediately implement a simple seven-step action plan to make an extra $100,000 in your business next year, minimum. That's right, no typo here, I said 6 figures. And, yes, I said minimum. Sounds like an info-mercial, right?

You don't have to imagine it; you will be able to do it if you keep reading.

This seven-step secret has been well-guarded, and never exposed in writing... until now. When I share the Simple 7 Step Action Plan with entrepreneurs, I see their eyes light up, and their bodies lean forward in their seats as they get ready to learn something that can boost their business to a whole new level. So sit back, relax, grab a tasty beverage, and I will share this secret with you.

One quick warning though: Once you learn this secret your business will never be the same, you will never look at adv the same and you will never look at your brand the same. You will be one of my Become an Award Winning Company (BAAWC) Rockstars and will launch your business to a new level of credibility, exposure, success, and status.

"Sure," you may say, "I've heard this before and then closed the book, only to find the author is full of you-know-what." I understand your concern. That's why, if you read this book, apply the 7 Step Action Plan, and aren't completely satisfied and convinced that this secret and this book are two of the most powerful tools in your business toolbox, then let me know and I will refund you your money. Sound good?

Before I give you my quick story, I would like to share how this book is arranged: The first part will explain why you should be reading it. In the next section, I introduce myself and my full entrepreneurial story. I then explain some fundamental things I have learned that are essential to know before I discuss the benefits of becoming an award-winning company.

Next, I explain why I wrote this book, and how to become part of the BAAWC Rockstar Community. The middle section explains the benefits of winning awards, and each one is supported by a corresponding interview with one of the nation's most well respected entrepreneurs. The end of the book explains the Simple 7 Step Action Plan to achieve award-winning company status in your business, and wraps up with a few tips that will help you in your journey to becoming an award-winning company.

My Quick Story

So now you may be thinking, "Who is this Matt guy anyway?" If you live outside of the Northern Colorado area, you probably don't know me at all. So let me take a moment to share my story. (I love sharing my experiences and stories with other entrepreneurs, and later I share my story more in depth. All the stories I mention about myself and M & E Painting come from my firsthand experiences in the trenches, and I am excited for you to read them.)

I have been an entrepreneur since the young age of 10. At this age, I learned how to create something from nothing; put my mind to something and see it through; and be creative and break the rules while others conformed...only to be told to sit down and shut up. After my passion was stifled for being an entrepreneur, I took the road more traveled of exchanging time for dollars, only to find that was a dead-end road.

When the spark was reignited for entrepreneurship my freshman year of college, I was hooked on the rush of the entrepreneurial ride once again. After making six figures in college, I graduated six figures in debt. College taught me many things, a lot having nothing to do with textbook knowledge. I learned how to make a lot of money (more on that "how" later on). I also learned the fiscal strategy the U.S. Government is using right now, which is to spend more than you make! Using this strategy left me in debt, but hey, at least I had a really nice car, school loans, and an overleveraged house to show for it.

I founded M & E Painting in 2005 with only $100 to my name. To date, M & E Painting has grown from a single Benjamin in the bank to a multimillion dollar industry leader. The company has served over 5,000 customers in seven years, bringing in more than $14 million in revenue, all while maintaining a 98% raving fan base that loves our company, its credo, its values, and its reason for being in business. Almost forgot to mention, we have won close two dozen business awards, and are regularly featured in the local, statewide, and national media!

But success doesn't come without some mistakes. The

only business course I ever took was the real-life "class" called "Lose $10,000 of My Own Money 101." But it was a real-life lesson that no college course could have taught me. I have learned other extremely valuable lessons, and am about to share many of them with you.

Let's Talk ROI

Being a lifelong entrepreneur, I know that one of the recurring questions business owners ask is how to get the best return on investment (ROI) for advertising. Over the past seven years of running my company, M & E Painting, I have spent close to a $1 million on advertising and marketing. Like many entrepreneurs, I am always tracking, calculating, readjusting, and tweaking my marketing and advertising mix to get the best ROI. This is a crucial task that all entrepreneurs must perform. Are you tracking your ROI?

Maximizing revenues and minimizing unneeded expenses, while still serving your customers extremely well, should be a goal of any entrepreneur. Over the past seven years, I have found the number one means to get the best ROI in any industry, and I guarantee that there is no less costly way to get any better results than the one I am about to share. Before I do, let's look at the marketing mix.

The Marketing Mix

I have advertised using direct mail, door knocking, cold calling, billboards, bus stops, bus benches, temporary tattoos, trade show booths, referral programs and incentives, radio, internet pay-per-click ads, search engine optimization programs and strategies, company lawn signs, fancy vehicle graphic wraps, and crazy dancing sign spinners standing on busy street corners (by the way, we have one of the country's best sign spinners—I challenge you to a dance off!). I have blogged, video blogged, networked, and advertised my name on shopping carts, and even urinals.

You name it, I have spent money on it. As I have continued to spend money on marketing and advertising, I have found the number-one, hands-down, best ROI on advertising that any entrepreneur can use in their business. It spans across all industries and is uniformly cheap and effective. Are you ready for the answer?

After all my research, tracking, and million bucks spent, the best ROI on advertising is, drum roll please...

None of Them

That's right, none of the $1 million I have spent on the above methods of "advertising" have brought me the ultimate, best ROI.

This is usually the part of my BAAWC presentation where the audience goes cross-eyed. "You just spent all this time telling me about ROI, your story, all the marketing you did, and what an 'expert' you claim to be, only to tell me none of it gave you the best ROI?"

"Absolutely," I respond, and then proceed to explain the truth about advertising.

CHAPTER 2

From Advertising to PR
with Dave Ramsey of The Lampo Group

The Truth About Advertising:
Nobody cares about what YOU say

The truth about advertising is summed up by the father-daughter marketing strategists Al Ries and Laura Ries in their book, *The Fall of Advertising & the Rise of PR*. They state that advertising has become more expensive, less effective, and more ignored over the years. We have been conditioned to take advertising at face value, which is a business owner's, or advertising agency's slanted, creative, funny, catchy, shocking, memorable, (fill in the adjective) way to get a customer to spend money with their company. The bigger truth is that it has ZERO credibility. A company is talking about itself when it advertises.

Maybe your company has the biggest, best, newest, most innovative, (again fill in the blank) product on the market. All your advertising is, is an attempt to get people to spend money with you.

Al and Laura state that advertising is not what builds a brand; PR is, and advertising reinforces it. They explain that advertising gives you no credibility (because it's your own words), while PR gives you ultimate credibility (because it is somebody else's words about you). Advertising is expensive, drains your cash, and leaves you less profit, while PR helps to sustain the long-term viability of your company, and allows you to become more profitable over time. PR is the tortoise, advertising is the hare.

I am not saying to stop your advertising entirely (because it does have an important place in your marketing plan), but understand WHY you are doing it, and WHERE and WHEN it will be most effective. Understand the true ROI on both advertising and PR, and make sure your investments in both are balanced and that you understand WHAT the functions of both are. I still advertise in my business, but now do it with a completely different understanding and mission of using it along with PR.

Your advertising vendors will not tell you this, because, well, they want to sell you advertising. They give you all kinds of reasons to do business with them:

- "You will get 10,000 exposures per dollar."
- "One job will pay back the cost of your ad."
- "We have the most opened direct mail package out there."
- "We can give you a tracking number to see which ad they called on."

Yes, these are all great ways you can get exposed, track call origination, get your money back, and so on and so forth, but ultimately all your advertisements do is reinforce the brand you have built. They do not build the brand. With PR, you can generate just as much exposure if not more, AND have it be 100% more credible while building your brand.

The Many Forms of PR

Just as advertising has many outlets, so does PR. The fundamental difference is who is sharing the message. With advertising, the business is sharing its message. With PR, it is somebody else.

PR can come in the form of newspaper, magazine, or print stories; blogs; articles; radio; TV; and awards. Remember, PR costs you no money. You do not pay the newspaper to write a story about you. If you do, you are buying an ad from their advertising department.

When a reporter writes a story about your business, that is PR. When my sign shaker stands on the corner and dances 'til he drops, you see the phone number on the sign, you call me, and I paint your house, advertising has served its purpose. When the *Denver Post* calls us to write a story about my sign shaker, or a high school student creates a Facebook page for him that now has close to 8,000 fans (the guy has more fans than me), that is PR. When I spend money to send a direct mail piece, or drop a door hanger in a neighborhood, that is advertising. When *Entrepreneur Magazine* writes a story about *M & E Painting's Free Paint Makeover*, that is PR.

How much would it have cost for us to run an ad of that magnitude in *Entrepreneur Magazine*? A whopping $83,480. A full-page color ad inside of *ColoradoBiz Magazine* costs $6,780. If they did advertise on the cover, I imagine the cost would be at least twice that. However, it cost us nothing when I was named by the same magazine as one of Colorado's Top 25 Most Influential Young Professionals in 2010 and my mug appeared on the cover.

So, all forms of PR have something in common: they are FREE. That said, you *will* spend time seeking out PR opportunities, contacting media outlets, pitching them, and building relationships. But you will never spend money for the story to come out.

My First Free PR Exposure

In 2007, we had a customer whose husband died suddenly of a heart attack. She called us around the holiday season to inform us of her tragic loss, and to express that she now couldn't afford to paint her house. I stopped by the very next day to return her deposit and give her a big hug. This particular customer was very much a promoter of our business in her community. She loved what we did, and what we stood for, and she helped me in my early years to get my name out in the community. After handing her the check and driving away from her house, I felt a sinking feeling in the pit of my stomach; I couldn't even begin to comprehend what it must be like to have such a tragic loss so unexpectedly.

That feeling lingered, and a few days later, my wife and I were driving though the neighborhood where she lived. Her house sat on the corner of a busy through street, and we had passed it many times before on our usual errand route. But after hearing this news, and driving by her house on this particular day, I was prompted to act. Her faded green house stuck out even more than it had before her loss, and her need was now more clear than ever.

I turned to my wife, Emily, and said, "Let's paint her house for free." Emily supported the idea, but wondered, "How can we do that, and what does that look like?" I explained that it didn't matter, we just needed to do it. She agreed, and that was the birth of our Free Paint Makeover Program. When we arrived back at our office just a few blocks away, I picked up the phone, called the customer, and informed her that we were going to paint her house free of charge.

In April 2008, our exceptional painting crew was out there making the house look brand new again. It turned out to be our favorite job of the year. When it was complete, the customer exited the house in tears, sharing with us how much it meant to her that we performed that act of kindness. The reason we decided to paint her house for free was because we knew it was the right thing to do. That woman and that house needed our help at that time in her life more than we ever needed the $3,300 we would normally charge.

Three weeks later, I was traveling with my wife, and my mom called me. I thought it was going to be another check-in to see if our-flight-was-okay-call. Instead, she exclaimed, "Matt, are you sitting down?" I immediately thought the worst.

I said, *"I am now, what's up?"*

"You are in the newspaper, that's what up."

Now let me ask you: If someone said those words to you, followed by silence, what is the first thing that would come to your mind? I scanned my brain, trying to think of all the reasons I could have been mentioned in the paper. My heart was pounding a million miles an hour, until I yelled, "For what?"

She read me these words from the April 19, 2008 *Thumbs Up Section* of the Fort Collins *Coloradoan* Newspaper:

Last fall, my husband and I had given Matt Shoup a deposit to have our house painted first thing in the spring. This past December, my husband had a heart attack and died suddenly. I contacted Shoup to tell him that I could no longer afford to paint my house. His response was to not only immediately send my deposit back, but to ask me if I would allow him to paint my house as a gift from him. He sent over his crew, they did an awesome prep and paint job, and my house looks gorgeous. I couldn't have gotten it done without Shoup's generosity. Thanks for my angel, Matt. A big thumbs up to Matt Shoup, Owner of M & E Painting.

The community I live in is not that big compared to major cities, yet it is big enough that it takes some good-sized news to make an impact and generate a reaction. As I flew home, my proud mom had already saved six or seven copies of the newspaper article, and had one already framed on her kitchen table.

Then the phone started to ring. It was previous customers, current potential customers, and even competitors calling to thank me, praise the company, and tell us how refreshing it was to read a story like that. And it wasn't really even a story, just a few sentences.

That was my first experience with PR. I did not intentionally follow any steps, action plan, or direction to contact the media, pitch them, and share a story; it was done for me. Little did I know that just a few months later, I would learn from a speaker and mentor I truly look up to, Cameron Herold (more on him in a minute), who would teach me how to become a PR machine, and alter the direction of my business forever. I met Cameron through a group I belong to called Entrepreneurs' Organization (EO), which has had a huge role in my molding and development as an entrepreneur.

The EO Impact

In late 2008, I accomplished a goal I had set for myself before I ever had my company. I wanted to join EO. It actually was Young Entrepreneurs' Organization (YEO) when I first heard about it at the age of 19. EO is a global network of entrepreneurs that are hand-selected by the EO board to join, after a rigorous interview and voting process. The majority of members are referred to the group, and I was able to attend and check out EO meet-and-greets, events, and get-togethers while in college before I even joined.

While attending Colorado State University (CSU), I worked for a company called College Works Painting (we'll come to back to this later). During those years, I was able to spend a lot of time with my first business mentor, Matt Landauer, the VP of the State of Colorado for College Works Painting. He was always talking about YEO, and how awesome it was. He went to events, retreats, speaking engagements, and participated in this "forum" thing that he couldn't really talk about or he would have to kill me. I was intrigued; from the outside it looked like a fraternity of super-successful businessmen and women, all of whom were officers or owners to some degree in businesses with annual revenues of a $1 million or more year after year.

Being a young and impressionable college kid, I was driven by money, and just the thought of running a $1 million company sounded cool! Little did I know that seven years after hearing about YEO, I would be inducted into EO. In 2007, the first year M & E Painting hit $1 million in revenue, I called one of the EO board members to inform him that I now qualified! I was the owner of a company that had hit the $1 million mark. The board member told me to make sure I did it again the following year, because the rule was that eligible companies need to show a history of at least $1 million in revenues for at least two years.

The way he said it challenged and inspired me to get that next million as quickly as possible. So, in May of 2008, I brought my P and L—which showed the company way above the half-way mark to $1 million for the year—to my CPA and she signed a letter to send in to the board. I called the board member to tell him I had done it, and then the journey with EO began.

The Junk Guy

One of the things I love most about EO is they know how to put on an event. They bring top talent from around the world to speak to business owners hungry to be inspired and grow their companies. The energy in a room filled with EOers is hard to explain unless you have been there. So, if you are reading this and are not a part of EO, check it out. If and when you join, remember to come back and re-read this section, and it will make more sense. Until then, just trust me.

Back to the events. I had been sent a notice by EO letting me know that Cameron Herold, the former COO of 1-800-GOT-JUNK, was coming to speak in Denver. Cameron is now the CEO of Back Pocket COO, and is an internationally sought-after business coach and speaker. He has recently released his book, *Double Double: How to Double Your Revenue and Profit in 3 Years or Less.* As I drove to Denver to listen to him speak, I was looking forward to the event, as I was strongly considering franchising my business. I was excited to hear his talk about how to grow my company.

Inside the hotel conference room, Cameron, in his cool and calm, yet commanding demeanor, explained how he had transformed 1-800-GOT-JUNK from a local Canadian business doing $2 million in annual revenue to an international brand bringing in $105 million in annual revenue, in six short years. One of his primary methods was commanding and directing a PR team that was purely dedicated to getting the media to write stories about the company. In five years, they had something ridiculous like 5,600 media stories (otherwise known as "hits") on their brand. Talk about free exposure.

Cameron then went on to tell the audience how much the company spent on traditional advertising, their marketing budget, and how that coincided with their PR plan. Guess how much they spent on advertising? Nothing! They spent $1,800 on obtaining franchisee leads over a few short years, but all of those 5,600 hits were absolutely unpaid for.

Going Out to Get Some PR

After listening to Cameron explain how easy PR was to obtain, I almost called him to ask him if he was crazy. There was no way it could be this easy. I held off on picking up the phone to call him, and instead picked up the phone to call some reporters; the results were astounding.

As described above, my first media hit was given to me in 2008, without any intervention on my part, by the Fort Collins

Coloradoan. This time, I called them, and pitched some amazing story ideas to them; the result was two back-to-back media hits, and my company and ugly mug on the front page of the business section of the *Coloradoan* in March of 2009.

I continued to work my newly learned systems and methods, and in no time was getting media hits left and right, all day long. It seemed every time I picked up the phone I got a hit. I was approaching Rockstar status, and my business was being featured all over the newspapers, in magazines, on TV, on the radio, and on the Internet—all with no cost to me.

An Interview With Dave Ramsey, CEO of The Lampo Group

In Part II, you will read several interviews with CEOs and other representatives from highly respected award-winning companies. Each of these interviews corresponds with a chapter describing a specific benefit of becoming an award-wining company. However, I wanted to share this one with you here. What Dave and I discussed is relevant to this topic of advertising vs. PR and how each has a role within lifting your brand.

It was an honor to sit down and share a phone call with a mentor and man I admire in the business world. Dave Ramsey is the CEO of The Lampo Group, a nationally known radio and TV personality, and a *New York Times* best-selling author of the books *Total Money Makeover* and *EntreLeadership*. Dave and The Lampo Group's mission is to provide "biblically based, common sense education and empowerment which gives HOPE to everyone from the financially secure to the financially distressed." [1]

The Lampo Group and Dave are both award winners,

and here is what Dave had to share about PR and his experience with winning awards.

More PR Means Less Advertising, But You Still Must Lift Your Brand With Style
Dave Ramsey: CEO, The Lampo Group
Nashville, TN
www.daveramsey.com

Matt Shoup: *Dave, great to talk to you, can we start off by you sharing the story of The Lampo Group being named* **Nashville Business Journal's** *Best Place to Work five years in a row?*

Dave Ramsey: *Sure, that particular award is put on by the* **Nashville Business Journal** *and has been for years. We were bumping along, had a great culture, and the PR team said, "Let's sign up for this thing."* **The Journal** *then sent out questionnaires to the team, and their feedback is what won the award. We always thought we were the best place to work, and it was great to have the award that says that.*

MS: *Awesome, what did you and The Lampo Group do to leverage the award? What did it do for the company?*

DR: *One way we leveraged the award was it made people jealous and want to work here. It attracted talent. The second big thing was that it tied into the* **EntreLeadership** *brand very well. This award gave credibility to what I teach entrepreneurs about hiring, company culture, and how you treat your team. This wasn't a primary brand touch point; yet at the same time it showed real true success.*

[1] See http://www.daveramsey.com/company/about-dave/

MS: *What were some lessons learned as you won this award and others?*

DR: *I have personally won lots of awards as well, because I am the brand. One thing I learned is that many of them are useless! One thing to consider is the weight the award carries. If the award is not bigger than you or bigger than those you are talking to, then who cares? I have won a lot of awards that I don't trumpet around because they don't lift me or my brand. Lesson being, the award needs to lift your brand.*

I was honored to win a **Marconi Radio Award** *after being nominated multiple times. That one sits here at our office because that is a huge award in the radio industry. This award was one that definitely gave me and my brand a lift.*

MS: *This is a perfect segue into my next question. As you talk about lifting your brand, explain a little more about how awards have done that, and also can you put a dollar amount on the exposure you believe awards have given your business?*

DR: *Sure, it is hard to say how many exact dollars these awards have lifted my brand. That's like asking the question, "what is the dollar amount of PR?" Another point to make is that awards and PR need to work hand in hand in a synchronizing fashion with your advertising as a strategic part of your total business plan to lift your brand with taste. We have an intention as to how we will do that and what awards, PR, and advertising play in that role. One thing is true, the more awards you win and PR you have, the less advertising you will need to do. At the same time, if all you do is win awards, it will start to sound pretty sickening pretty quick.*

MS: *Dave, you bring up the categories of PR and advertising. What have you seen to be the biggest differences between the two for you?*

DR: *PR has an instant credibility to it, and readers will put up less shield. When I read an article versus read an ad, I believe it more, even if it may not be true. Another thing is PR is a lot more trouble and time intensive to land than advertising, but there is no question it is a powerful brand building tool. The other great thing is that other than the time, payroll, and effort you put in, it's absolutely free!*

MS: *What other advice would you have for entrepreneurs looking to win awards and use this as part of their game plan?*

DR: *One thing, if you are going to seek an award, make sure it relates very specifically to your brand and is recognizable by your customers. **The Best Place to Work Award** took on new life as we launched the **EntreLeadership** brand. If you are going to go through the trouble of doing this intentionally as part of your overall strategic business plan, make sure you target a customer base for a desired result. It can't just be like, "Hey, I didn't get a trophy as a kid and I need one now." Have intention and a desired outcome.*

*Also, make sure the award means something real to your customer segment. Just because you get on as many magazine covers as you can means nothing. If you are a bankruptcy attorney and you make a magazine cover, it only holds weight in the bankruptcy attorney industry. Same with radio, that cover only means something in the radio realm. I would never go to a book publishing convention and tout my **Marconi**.*

MS: *Dave, this time had been great. Any last minute points, lessons, or things you would like to share?*

DR: *Yes, one more thing. Many business owners fall victim to the same thing I did. Entrepreneurs are all so result-and task-oriented that we don't care about the trophy; this can be a mistake. When the PR team first approached me about the **Best Place to Work Award**, I said "Whoopee, no big deal if we win, I already know we are a great place to work." My team said, "Hey this matters," and I said, "Sure, do it." When I was nominated for the **Marconi** five times and didn't win, we blew off the idea. I blew off the fact that these awards have value and give our brand a lift. The time spent in searching for and winning awards is worth it, and I honestly didn't know that at the time. It wasn't until I looked back after the fact and saw the result that I realized this.*

Hindsight Is Always 20/20

It would have been great to hear about all this free PR stuff before I dropped a million in marketing dollars. In all honesty, the million bucks I have spent in advertising I would rather have kept to myself; even half of it would have been nice. Think about all the free houses we could paint, people I could help, scholarships I could fund.

Guess what? I am on a plane as these words are being put down, while I work on my passion of inspiring entrepreneurs. If I had saved a little of that million, maybe I would be in first class as I fly to Spain.

That's right, I am 30,000 feet high above the Atlantic (and this "ain't no short flight!") and, man, is my back sore, crammed up in coach! Well, I am actually stretched out over three seats because the flight was far from booked, but this lady keeps leaning her seat back and banging me in the head as I try to type. Hold on, check this out: Up in the first class cabin, some guy just got a nice hot towel for his face. I'm just lucky not to get hit by the drink cart as it rolls by…watch those elbows and knees! Mimosas, what?! He just got a mimosa… okay coach really stinks. I got a warm Coke! Just use PR, and chill out a little on the advertising, it's just not as effective. Save some of that money and fly first class. Your legs will thank you!

CHAPTER 3

My Why

Back to being serious, I want to share why I do what I do. When I started writing this book, I knew that I was going to expose a secret to you that would allow you to be empowered in your business. I knew that I would teach you lessons from my stories and experiences and share my "ah-ha" moments, and help you prevent making the same mistakes I did. So, yes, I am going to show you what to do and how to do it, but I first want to explain why I am doing it.

Another life changing presentation I had the opportunity to attend through EO was from Simon Sinek, the author of *Start With Why*. Simon captivated me and the audience one evening by stating, "People don't buy what you do, they buy why you do it." He is the WHY guy, and is rolling around the globe, inspiring action in the business world, governments, organizations, and (I am sure) anyone who reads his books or listens to him speak.

Once I found my WHY, I was on fire. So here is WHY I am writing this book: **to inspire as many entrepreneurs as I can before I die, and even after.** I am not talking about the short lived "rah-rah" session; I mean you will close this book and continue to be truly inspired day after day, week after week, month after month, and year after year. I know God put me on this planet and gave me the gifts he did so

I could inspire business leaders. This book comes at a time when entrepreneurs have the ability to drastically change the economy, the country, and the world. This is a crucial time in the nation's history, a time when legends will be made. I will be one of those legends to bring true positive change to this country and the world.

The Heart of Every Entrepreneur

I am a capitalist and entrepreneur at heart. I believe in capitalism to its core, and fundamentally support it. I am a big believer in getting up every day, going out, making things happen, and, as Dave Ramsey says, "leaving the cave, killing something, and bringing it home." I have tried to rely on others and work for "the man" to support my family and make my dreams happen, and it just didn't work for me. I am guessing that if you are an entrepreneur reading this book, you feel the same way.

The next thing I am sure you may agree with me on is that entrepreneurs choose the life and the road less traveled in order to have freedom. Having freedom can mean many things. It can mean having the time to do the things you enjoy. It can also mean having the financial freedom to leave a legacy for your family.

This could come in the form of a "lifestyle business." For example, I have a good friend who has a hardwood floor business. He seems to have found the balance between small, consistent revenue, and the highest margin of profit available for his company. He tried the route of big revenues, big growth, and high overhead, only to find he made the same amount of money to support his lifestyle, BUT he had a lot more headaches. Now, he has rid his business of all that, and still has the time and financial freedom to live the life he wants to live.

Some entrepreneurs may be on the track of growing their companies to flip, sell, merge, take public, and receive a big payday. From that they may go buy an island and retire, reinvest into another business, and do the same thing over and over... or do a little of both.

Point being that we all have different desired outcomes and visions for our businesses, yet our fundamental belief as entrepreneurs is that we control our destiny. This destiny will not be left in the hands of others, such as employers, the government, or that old rich uncle who is leaving a big inheritance for us.

I am also sure we can agree that entrepreneurs love the challenges of taking something and making it grow, growing from challenges, and reaping the rewards and benefits from a job well done. We are also willing to take accountability and responsibility for the fact that we can screw up and it will cost us in the short term, yet grow us in the long term. We are ultimately responsible for all that happens in our business, and never blame, make excuses, or deny what happens when it does happen.

These are the people I am inspiring and serving, and in doing so I am also creating a community of BAAWC Rockstars.

What Is a BAAWC Rockstar?

A BAAWC Rockstar is an entrepreneur who holds true to the fundamentals of entrepreneurship. He or she has a vision, takes it, and runs with it. BAAWC Rockstars don't get a bailout if they screw up, just a nice kick in the butt. After that, they get back up and go for it again. They hit it big, and deserve every penny they earn, because they served a bunch of people with excellence—people like their customers, team members, vendors, and community at large. They don't need to see the profit on the P and L before being willing to make the leap to go and make that profit happen. They don't need evidence before belief; they have faith that their abilities, efforts, and actions will make them rich.

They are constantly seeking to improve themselves, their companies, and their futures. They support and encourage others who do the same thing, learning from people who have been there and done that, and teaching others who want to follow in their footsteps. A BAAWC Rockstar never backs down from a challenge, and seeks to grow and learn by shooting for the stars. If they miss, they still hit the moon, while the people around them only try to jump for the sky.

A BAAWC Rockstar knows how lonely it can be at the top, and seeks to build relationships with other BAAWC Rockstars (that's why I created the www.baawc.com website and blog, to unite BAAWC Rockstars). People outside the BAAWC Rockstar Community may see them as crazy, as they go left when many go right. They are innovators and admired when that craziness and innovation becomes the norm that the rest of the crowd follows years later. By then, they are on to more innovation and always living and dreaming years ahead of the crowd.

BAAWC Rockstars run their businesses and lives with integrity, honesty, and service. They stand up for what's right, no matter what, and whether somebody is or isn't looking. They take ultimate ownership and accountability for all they do, and all that results from their actions, good or bad. They never take the road of blaming or making excuses.

So that's a BAAWC Rockstar. If that is you, and you are in, I would be honored if you would join the Community with me (completely free of course!), the official founder and world's first member of the BAAWC Rockstar Community. Just go to **www.baawc.com** and click on the star on the homepage to join!

When you read this book and apply the principles and the Simple 7 Step Action Plan I teach, I want to hear from you about it, and help others to learn from your successes. As a bonus, you will receive the *BAAWC Official Workbook* that accompanies this book. In it, you will find the exercises listed in the following chapters, as well as many other prompts to help you get ready to become an award-winning company. You will also receive invitations to contribute to my weekly blog, which is designed to help other Rockstars in the community, and as an added bonus - it will give you tons of free exposure for your company.

What It Means to Be a BAAWC Rockstar

Entrepreneurs are the glue that holds this country together, and we need more empowered, inspired, and forward thinking entrepreneurs in this world. We need to be connected to each other, and know how to get in touch with each other, in order to support each other in times of success and abundance, as well as times of need and distress.

We need to make some real changes in the economy, and I know we can do it. I always say, 'Never underestimate an entrepreneur.' When somebody tells me I can't do something, I go do it, just to prove them wrong. When I am passionate about something wholeheartedly, I can't be stopped. I also want to build the BAAWC Rockstar Community to help each other, serve each other, inspire each other to do great things, and live the entrepreneurial good life. This book is not just about winning awards, it is about leading a world wide community of entrepreneurs to take massive action and change the course of history! Let's do this, Rockstars!

CHAPTER 4

Becoming an Award Winning Company

The Rest of This Book

Now, let's shift gears and get into this big secret I have been talking about. How do you become an award-winning company? Why would you want to do this, and how do you do it? Meaning just what exactly do you need to do daily to make it happen? And, how about a little proof from somebody other than me to show you it actually works? You'll find it all here.

In the next chapter, I will share my story as an entrepreneur, beginning with my first company, which I founded at the age of 10. Remember, I already gave you the CliffsNotes version, but will now share the details, showing you how I became a BAAWC Rockstar and why I want to help others do the same.

From there, I will share the benefits of being an award-winning company, backed by stories from their leaders. I will then share the 7 Simple Steps for you to follow and take action on today.

As you read through this book you will see boxed off sections at the end of certain chapters or sections of chapters titled WORKING IT OUT. These boxes are the same questions you will find in the free workbook you received when you joined the Rockstar Community. You can stop after each section to contemplate the questions or read through the entire book first and then go through the workbook. The workbook is an editable PDF that you can save to your computer to continue to build and work on as you immerse yourself in the awards process.

Whether you use the WORKING IT OUT sections in this book, or use the workbook, going through these questions will help you prepare to win awards by responding to questions typically posed in award applications.

The Interviews

Don't just take my word for it! As you read through these chapters, you will hear from some of the country's most well-respected and successful award-winning CEOs, entrepreneurs, and leaders, who share how they did the same thing I did. In the following interviews, these well-known businessmen and women share their stories of when and how they achieved their award-winning company status and what is has done for their business.

These interviews truly inspired me, and I hope they will inspire you. I intentionally interviewed CEOs from different industries, from companies with different revenue levels, and numbers of employees to show how this applies to any and every entrepreneur. Depending on your goals and the nature of your company, you might find some of the interviews more applicable to your situation than others. One thing you will find in all of them is inspiration from these business leaders reaching new levels of success.

If you don't see your industry represented here, don't

worry. Did you know there is a scholarship for a left handed, first generation, curly haired high school student who wants to study biology on a remote island in the Pacific? Likewise, there is an award for just about every business and industry, no matter how obscure or unique, so get ready to win it! First, here are a few quick tips:

Your Team

If you are a larger company and have a PR team, you will want to share this book with them. These seven steps are simple, teachable and duplicatable. Once you have read this book, plan on having your PR department do the same. If you are your own PR department, then you are ready to go as soon as you close this book.

Set Goals

After you read this book, I am sure you will be ready to jump right in and start winning awards immediately. In order to measure, set and attain success, be sure to apply some goals to this process. What specific awards would you like to apply for, win, and by when? What will these awards mean to your company, and how will you leverage them to do business? Like anything, don't do it blind and with no planned outcome. Having a written goal and accomplishing it will give you that satisfaction that you are on track, and hold you and your company accountable.

When I first learned this secret, and was named a finalist, but not a winner, for an award in December of 2009, I decided I wanted to win our first Colorado based award by the end of June 2010, and to win our first national award by the end of 2010. Make sure if you are setting goals that they are realistic and attainable. You may have seen the acronym SMART when it comes to goal setting:

Specific. Is your goal specific as to what award or type of award you want to win?

Measurable. Can you measure the number of applications you have filled out, searches you have conducted, and how many you must apply for to win?

Attainable. Are you actually able to win the award being applied for in the time you set? Be sure you are setting yourself up for success by carefully reviewing award criteria as you set goals.

Realistic. Once you view the criteria for a particular award, ask yourself if it can realistically be applied for and won.

Timely. Put a time stamp on everything. Write down a specific date that you want to accomplish these applications and win these awards.

Think About Your Elevator Pitch

As we talked about earlier, advertising is becoming more expensive and less effective every day. One of the reasons is that the sheer volume of messages is overwhelming. We train ourselves to avoid these messages as they scream for our attention while we drive to the office, surf the web, click through the TV, and go about our daily lives.

At networking events and when being introduced to new people, you need a memorable way to grab people's attention. Here is where the elevator pitch comes in. You'll have 30 to

60 seconds to deliver your pitch, but in reality, you only have about three to five seconds to make an impact. If you don't, then you are just one more among the impactless commercials, billboards, and other media screaming for people's attention.

A pitch might go something like this:

"I'm Gerald. I love making people love their homes, by taking their dream for a basement and making it a reality. Gerald's Basement Refinishing and Remodeling is a local family owned business, and we specialize in remodeling and refinishing basements in the Denver metro area. I'm passionate about building and design, and I love to share my expertise and knowledge to make my customers' dreams happen. Have you been dreaming about your basement lately?"

Did he grab your attention quickly? Was it unique? Yeah, it was pretty good, but remember that advertising is a company talking about itself. Gerald was just talking about himself.

What if he could add this:

"You don't have to take my word for it. For three years in a row, the *Denver Business Journal* has recognized us as one of Denver's Fastest Growing Companies. Last year, *ColoradoBiz Magazine* named us a *Colorado Company to Watch*, and this year, we were a finalist for a *Stevie Award* for the nation's *Best Overall Small Company of the Year!*"

Being an award-winning company gives Gerald's elevator pitch power and credibility. His pitch is backed up by third parties that support what he says. You don't have to take a company's word for it (advertising), when they are award-winning. Other credible organizations and people are talking about the company, and this is powerful.

WORKING IT OUT

Create your own company pitch. What is the 30 to 60 second attention-grabber that will get people interested in doing business with you? How are you turning heads within five seconds? How are you addressing and solving a problem? Can anyone else back up your claims?

Write your pitch and practice it with friends and team members. Just the exercise of doing this is the first step in becoming comfortable with talking about your company. You will be amazed at how it prepares you be at ease and speak naturally with others about your company. It's also great practice for when you start to write about your company on award applications.

CHAPTER 5

It's Story Time

My First Business

In 1991, I was 10 years old. My family had just moved to Loveland, Colorado, from Montclair, New Jersey. I remember sitting in my basement bedroom listening to the radio, trying to record songs onto cassette tapes for my Walkman. As much as I loved doing that, I also saw lots of my friends listening to CDs. My $4 weekly allowance went straight to muscling up my baseball card collection and, at $200, a CD player (let alone CDs for it) was far outside my financial reach.

So I asked Mom and Dad to buy me one, and their answer was clear: "We aren't buying you a $200 CD player. Do you think money grows on trees? If you want a CD player, go find a way to make $200." Little did they know how those words would stick with me and that they had officially inspired me to become an entrepreneur. "Go find a way," they said. That's the beauty of entrepreneurship: We have the ability to go out and make something happen—take an idea, and make some money with it.

I didn't whine and complain about them not buying me the CD player; rather, I asked them a question: "Can I borrow your lawnmower?"

I went around my neighborhood asking neighbors if I could mow their grass for fifteen or twenty bucks. How could they resist the charm of a skinny, buck-toothed youngster standing at their door? I built up a small base of regular customers and began to learn the basic principles of scheduling; setting, managing, and delivering on client expectations; establishing recurring revenues; and keeping customers happy. At the end of the summer, I was pumped to go into the store with my parents and hand over my hard-earned money to purchase that CD player. This is one of the first memories I have of setting, mapping out, focusing on, and achieving a goal.

But, I now had another problem—what to do with the extra money. I had made $200 quickly, and now had a few hundred more.

When school started, I realized the school store was the happening place for students to purchase snacks and hang out. On a family shopping trip to the local bulk warehouse store, I calculated that an $8 box of 50 candy bars made each bar only 16 cents. The school store was selling them for 60 cents! Light bulb! With the extra money I had made from lawn mowing, I purchased boxes of snacks and started my second business—peddling candy out of my locker for less than the school store sold them for. My parents' joke now is that if we had stayed in New Jersey, I would have ended up peddling something else! Threatened with suspension, I shut down my second business within weeks of its start, but not before making a bunch of money and learning additional business concepts, including profit, repeat business, marketing and sales, and the importance of having a business plan.

(Oh yeah, and governmental regulations of business.)

I never asked for another allowance or handout again, but I found that the schools stifled my passion for entrepreneurship. So, for the next few years, I gave up on it, and instead earned money through exchanging my time for dollars. I wasn't a fan of this equation, and saw it as a dead end. If I wanted more money, I had to work more hours, and that was it. In my high school years, I worked as a busboy at a friend's family's restaurant, a salesman at a shoe store, and an assistant manager at a fast-food restaurant. I was proud of the car I purchased, the clothes I put on my own back, and the extracurricular activities I participated in with my own hard earned money. Upon graduation, I was accepted to Colorado State University, where my passion for entrepreneurship was reignited.

The Opportunity

I often struggled, after a long weekend of "collegiate endeavors," to make my 8:00 am Monday Biology class. One particular Monday, I felt motivated and inspired to pull myself out of bed, blast through the cafeteria, and run across campus to my first class of the day. Before the professor began his lecture, he gave over the floor for a quick announcement about a summer internship. "Wonderful," I thought, "loads of work for zero money. Here we go."

The speaker, Jeff, was the campus recruiter for College Works Painting. As an intern his first year, he had done so well that the company had promoted him to this position. You could tell he was a successful, confident, and excellent entrepreneur. Here is what he announced:

"Hey guys, before you tune me out about this internship, I just want you to know that the one I am offering is a little different than what you might think. Why? Because I made $19,000 last summer. I am here looking for students who would like to learn how to run a business with someone else's money, and have the opportunity to make anywhere from $3,000 to $30,000 this summer. If this is for you, fill out this card."

I didn't hear anything else other than **$19,000**, and **run a business**. I was accustomed to working hard and making good money. I had always been very driven and competitive, and I figured that if this guy made $19,000, I could make more. (No offense, Jeff) I went through an extensive recruiting and interview process to be selected as an intern, and three months later I was knee-deep in the business of painting houses.

I learned about forming a business plan, sales, marketing, hiring, interviewing, production, painting, and customer service. I was thrilled as my entrepreneurial flame was reignited. The spring and summer of 2000, was one of the most challenging, yet rewarding periods of my life. My comfort zone was expanded, and I was thrown out of it daily. Six months earlier I had no idea how to open a paint can, let alone run a painting company. I ended the summer as a top intern with one of the nation's highest selling and producing painting branches and, oh yeah, I made a cool $23k.

For the next three years, I was a district manager and campus recruiting intern. I learned about the company management levels by working as a district manager and recruiting and training new branch managers. Painting is not a glamorous business, but it is the business they used to teach me about business. I figured I would take the experience I learned with painting and transfer it to another industry.

I now had the passion to be a business owner again, but there was a problem: I had made over six figures painting houses in college, but also spent that six figures, plus another six figures. So, I was in debt close to $100,000. I had earned way more than my college cohorts, but for all the business training I had received, I hadn't learned the basic equation of money in versus money out in my personal spending.

Of the $100,000 plus that I had made while painting in college, I had nothing in the bank to show for it. I married my college sweetheart, Emily, and we settled down in Fort Collins. I should have been worried sick, but I was not. I was about to jump on the train many were boarding at the time. It was headed to the land of luxury, abundance, and wealth, but with corruption, greed, and deceit at its core. I am talking about the mortgage train, and I jumped right on.

The Not-So-Sexy Mortgage Business

I met a man who was doing very well in the mortgage business and I was inspired to follow in his footsteps and enter this profession. I was a guy who knew how to make lots of money and figured this was a way to do it. I saw my friend and others in the business closing deals and making hundreds of thousands of dollars, and I wanted in. I entered the mortgage business in 2003, and was immediately shocked at how deals were getting done. Some of the customers were getting royally screwed.

I remember hearing a corporate trainer teach the "art" of rooting out those people who had debt and equity in their homes. He explained the process of tying their unsecured credit card debt into their home mortgage for payments over 30 years in order to "save" on monthly payments. He even pulled verses from the Bible to validate his claims of what great things we were doing for people. When he was finished, I inquired whether we might instead teach people how to avoid debt altogether ('cause the Bible says that too). The manager and top producer in this company replied, "Do you want to make some f*#@! money or just ask a lot of questions? Because you can't do both. If you want to get rich, don't ask so many questions. Just close the deals."

As he slammed Red Bulls and stormed around the office flexing his muscles and screaming at suits to close deals, he reminded me of one of the coked-out meatheads portrayed in the movie Boiler Room. (If you haven't seen the movie Boiler Room, go watch it to see what not to do with your life.) This manager's lovely strategy soon put him, and everyone else in that industry, out of a job when the mortgage train derailed, crashed and burned.

By mid-2004, I had made my way to the more conservative side of the money world as a bank mortgage officer. Talk about a change of scenery! I was immediately surprised by the way this bank operated. There was a sincere concern for the well-being of clients—ensuring that the loan they were offered was a loan they could afford.

This way of doing things also included a lot of processes and paper trails. So I had now had my taste of both sides of the mortgage spectrum. Neither ignited a passion to continue in the industry, but in my mind I had no choice. A passionless career seemed the only way to support my family, pay my bills, and get out of debt. But I just knew there was something better for me around the corner.

I approached that corner one day in March of 2005, when the new manager of the bank's mortgage division called me into his office. What I thought was a talk about my future with the bank, I quickly realized was not. He explained that my future with the bank ended that day, because he was letting me go. "Maybe you should go do that painting thing," he said with a smirk.

I was blindsided. I was young, broke, and in debt, with no source of income. Yet, losing that job was the best thing that ever happened to me. That was my turning point. I vowed I would never be a slave to a boss again, and I left the office ready to become a BAAWC Rockstar.

The M & E Painting Story

I walked through the door of my overleveraged condo in Fort Collins and announced, "Honey, I'm home. I got let go today!" Emily had been working full-time at an elder care facility. Her income took care of the basics, but my check was the bulk of our earnings and absolutely necessary for our survival. Robert Kiyosaki, author of *Rich Dad, Poor Dad* and other books about wealth, suggests that a great determiner of wealth is to stop working and see how long your money lasts. We knew that our wealth was going to dry up pretty quickly. We had $100 to our name. We used it that day for the minimum requirement to open a business checking account.

I immediately went out into my neighborhood and began knocking on doors once again. This time, the stakes were higher than just a CD player. My family, our future, our home, and my dignity were all on the line. I needed to make almost $3,000 in twenty-five days in order to pay the mortgage, put food on the table, and keep the lights on. Failure was not an option.

After a few hours of knocking on doors, I had my first customer. I still run into Cindi every few months, and I can't thank her enough for putting her faith and trust in me. Cindi asked the name of my company. The first thing that came to my mind was the initials of my and my wife's first names, and M & E Painting was born.

After purchasing some business cards, vehicle signs, and estimate forms, our business account went down from $100 to $25. Then I closed that first deal, and then a few more. I hired my first crew, and then my second. I practiced daily income-producing action steps such as prospecting, going on sales appointments, and making connections and contacts by telephone, email, and anywhere else I could.

At the end of 25 days, I had my $3,000, and by the end of 2005, we had painted 200 houses and profitably produced over $500,000 worth of business. We were now able to breathe and hold our heads above water. We paid down some personal debt and reinvested in the business. In 2006, we did almost $800,000 in revenue. In 2007, we pushed over the $1 million mark, and by 2009, we were at $2 million.

As the years passed, we gained momentum, and (after following the PR steps I learned from that EO event) started to be noticed by the local press and media. From 2005 through 2013, M & E Painting painted over 5,000 homes in Colorado, producing a total of roughly $14 million in paint jobs while maintaining a 98.6% customer satisfaction rating. We became known as the company seen everywhere because of our unique, consistent, and aggressive "guerilla marketing" efforts. Again, close to $1 million spent in marketing trial-and-error only to find out none of it was the best way to go about building our brand.

Fast forward to the present (late 2013, as I revise this). M & E Painting, and myself as President, have been named finalists and/or winners of 24 awards in the past 4 years. Companies and organizations like *Inc. Magazine*, *Winning Workplaces*, *The American Business Awards*, *ColoradoBiz Magazine*, local Chambers of Commerce, and the *Northern Colorado Business Report*, have bestowed on us the awards *Fastest Growing*, *Best Place to Work*, and *Top Young Professional*, just to name a few (check out the full awards list in Appendix I).

At the end of 2009, after being nominated for my first award, I learned the **million dollar secret** of how awards can lead to business success. I then created an action plan of 7 Simple Steps to implement into my business strategy. I immediately saw the benefits, dispelled the myths, and leveraged these awards for the growth of our company. I am now going to show you how to do the same thing.

This secret has become so essential to the success of my business and can be just as valuable for any entrepreneur in any industry. How would you like to:

- Gain and retain significantly more revenue and profits
- Have potential customers coming to you instead of the other way around
- Stop wasting money on advertising
- Win free press and media exposure
- Obtain local, state, national, and even international exposure
- Land the opportunity to rub elbows with other entrepreneurial and business elites
- Be considered an expert in your industry

Of course you would like this! These are just a few of the benefits of becoming an award-winning company and this is what Part II of the book will cover.

This WORKING IT OUT section will help you craft your story, which will be crucial to implementing one of the 7 Simple Steps.

WORKING IT OUT

- What is your story? Write out your entrepreneurial story; include the ups, downs, goods, bads, and uglies. What were the moments, experiences, and people that shaped the journey?
- What is the importance of telling your story in your business?
- Why do your customers need to hear your story?
- How about your team, vendors, friends, family, investors, etc.?
- What traits did you receive from your parents, peers, or role models growing up?
- How have those people and their ways affected your business today?

- How do you feel these traits will help you to become an award-winning company?
- What were some of your childhood goals?
- How did goal setting shape your entrepreneurial ventures today?
- What is your vision? Is it clearly described? If not, take some time to write the vision for your company.

Don't worry about specific goals yet. Just describe your company as you see it in the future. Having a vision for your business is crucial for becoming an award-winning company. Once you have your vision down, write more specifically about the awards portion of this vision:

- How does being an award-winning company fit into the vision of your company?
- What awards are you winning?
- How are customers, vendors, and team members reacting to these awards?
- How is your business leveraging these awards for more revenue and profits?
- What does the winning of these awards do for your culture, morale, and public image?

PART II:

Benefits of Winning Awards and Examples of How Companies Have Done So and Leveraged Their Awards for Success

CHAPTER 6

The Benefit of Building Your Brand with Curt Richardson and Kristen Tatti of OtterBox

Before I go into the benefits of being an award-winning company, I want to make one thing clear: You can be a crappy company and still win awards. Unfortunately, bad companies can sneak under the radar and win an award or two but if, at their core, they have no integrity, lack accountability, and demonstrate all the other things that bad companies bring, they will not last long. In Part IV, I outline the top things I know will make your company a killer company. The idea is that your company speaks for itself, and the award is just there to support it. Don't go win an award and think it will fix your company if it is broken in any way, because it will not.

This first interview with Curt Richardson, CEO of OtterBox, demonstrates this point very well. Curt also talks about how winning awards can help you build your brand. I have already mentioned that awards, as a leg of PR, are beneficial for building your brand. Not only will your brand be built by awards, but it will become stronger if you are already a great company.

I first heard about OtterBox when I was in a Best Buy looking at cell phone cases. This was late 2009. Within six months of hearing about them for the first time, I couldn't get away from their name. From their massive media and press coverage to their involvement in the community, their explosive growth, and, oh yeah, they have won tons of awards too. Curt Richardson and OtterBox have made a huge impact on the Northern Colorado community, and they are just getting started.

I was honored to sit down with Curt to find out what role awards have played in the growth of his company and global brand. Curt started from a shop in his garage 12 years ago, and has grown OtterBox into a multimillion dollar company. I followed up with Kristen Tatti in OtterBox's PR and Media department. I was also honored to spend time with Kristen to hear her take on how awards being a key piece of the company's PR efforts.

Build Your Brand But Let Your Company Speak for Itself
Curt Richardson: CEO, OtterBox
Fort Collins, CO
www.otterbox.com

Matt Shoup: *Thank you so much for meeting with me. OtterBox has been making huge waves over the past few years in a very positive way. Can you tell me the OtterBox story, and touch on how winning awards has helped the company?*

Curt Richardson: *Sure! We started our business years ago doing injection molding and selling those products to other companies. We then decided that we wanted to create, brand, and distribute our own products, and started doing so. We have been doubling revenues year over year, and expect to continue to do so for the next* five years. Awards have played a large role in our business and PR plan. It seems like we are winning two to three big ones each year.

MS: *So, what benefits have these award brought to the company?*

CR: It gets the team excited to work for an up-and-coming, forward-thinking company. It is a huge morale booster and helps to build the culture of OtterBox. Another big thing is that it gets the name out there. Part of our business plan and strategy when it comes to marketing is that we do not invest in traditional marketing, such as TV, radio, and print ads. We approach it more as trying to brand ourselves with PR. This is a lot less expensive and builds a stronger brand, although it may take longer to do. Awards have played a large role in getting this exposure.

Our PR team works on gaining free media exposure as well as applying for and winning awards. When we receive these awards and PR exposure, it lets more people know about us and what we are doing. We are trying to build a worldwide brand, and all this exposure helps.

MS: *You mentioned that you are a guy who likes to stay out of the limelight. Tell me how this comes into play when you are being recognized for such prestigious awards.*

CR: I am a big believer that your company needs to speak for itself. If it does, then the award is just the extra accolade that confirms it. Don't get me wrong, it is an honor to receive these awards, but it is not about the award or me. The awards and recognition are great, but if your company is not congruent with the award you receive, the company can be portrayed as being hypocritical. The awards are not about me; they are about OtterBox and the wonderful, innovative company that was created by each member of our team. I couldn't have done this without them.

MS: *Tell me a little more about the phrase, "Let the company speak for itself."*

CR: *As I mentioned, awards are just a small part of our business plan. I think it is important for a company to have a clearly defined vision and culture and to know what part winning awards will play in that. I also feel that the company must execute and deliver on that plan—especially when it comes to satisfying customers. We live in such a "now" society, where the power of the Internet, social media, and exposure to instant information is there. This can make or break a company if they are or aren't doing a good job for their clients. So, awards are not important if a company is not delivering. When I say, 'Let the company speak for itself,' I mean let it do just that by its service, values, and delivering on its promises with precision. It makes no sense to be an award-winning company if you are not doing this. Then you look like a hypocrite to your customers and those around viewing what you are doing.*

MS: *What would you say the return is on the time and energy your team puts into winning awards for OtterBox?*

CR: *The return is easily ten-fold.*

MS: *What does this return look like in tangible value to OtterBox?*
  CR: *The return comes in many forms. One is obviously the credibility and name recognition, and exposure in the media, papers, magazines, etc., but more so is the attraction of people who*

want to work on the OtterBox team, who are a great fit for our culture. Lastly is the vibe and energy that it creates within the company. The morale boost is something that has contributed to better productivity and a more inspired team.

MS: *What advice would you give to entrepreneurs looking to win awards for their businesses?*

CR: *First of all, let your company speak for itself, and make sure your company can back up the award you are attempting to win. You need to perform better than a company that is not an award-winning company. Think about your company's vision, direction, and overall goals, and ask yourself what role winning awards plays in this master plan. Also, remember that once you become an award-winning company, you and your company will be put on a pedestal and you will be in the limelight more than others. With this will come great connections, meeting other entrepreneurs, and other good things. With this will also come multiple solicitations and approaches for you to get involved with things you may not want to do. Just remember to know why you are applying for the award, and make sure you have a team, company, and brand that support it.*

Focus on Quality
Kristen Tatti: PR Department, OtterBox
Fort Collins, CO
www.otterbox.com

Matt Shoup: *Tell me a little about your role within OtterBox in the specific department of PR.*

Kristen Tatti: *We are in charge of attaining media and PR exposure for the company. Part of this plan is to strategically search and apply for awards. This is easy work for us because OtterBox is such a great company to work for. Curt basically built the company and its story, and I just get to brag to the public and press about it!*

MS: *What do you see as being the biggest part of OtterBox's success?*

KT: *With all of the attention we have been receiving for our growth, some people do not know that this company started in Curt's garage. He was a serial entrepreneur and had many failures before the growth and success of OtterBox. I say that Curt saw entrepreneurial success when he focused on something he was passionate about. That was when it started to grow at a rapid pace. The OtterBox team has made it a point to work toward our passions while still listening to what the customer wants and needs.*

MS: *OtterBox has applied for some awards that have requested in-depth information about the inner workings of the company. Tell me about that process.*

KT: *One of the awards we were nominated for was a best workplace award. We had to collaborate interdepartmentally.*

When we finished our research and findings to report for this award, we had an 11-page document that was available for reference and future use.

I think an important thing for business owners, or their PR department, is to know is that initial applications for the first awards applied for will be very time consuming. There is a lot of learning about yourself and the company to be done while you are applying. Once you have this information, it is very easy to evolve, change, and adapt it over time. So, my advice is to take the time initially to make it great, and then continue to build on that for each award the company applies for.

MS: *What other advice would you give to entrepreneurs looking to win awards?*

KT: *Focus on quality not quantity. We use the sniper rifle approach versus the shotgun approach when it comes to searching and applying for awards. We focus on awards we really think we can win, and have actual proof that we deserve to win! If we think we are not ready for a particular award, we do not apply for it.*

Another piece of advice is to build your list of media contacts. The media has been especially helpful in wanting to know about awards won, and wanting to spread the news!

WORKING IT OUT

- What are the biggest challenges your business is facing right now? Be specific.
- How is the economy affecting you?
- Are your revenues up, down, or static?
- What is the state of your profits, sales ratios, and closing ratios? (Sales ratios are the number of jobs you win divided by the number of jobs you bid on. Keep in mind there is usually an industry average that you can compare to. You may ask others in the same field or industry what is an average ratio. To be an award-winning company, your sales ratio must be better than average.)
- Have these ratios been increasing? Decreasing?
- What is your competition up to?
- Are you seeing any shifts or changes in your industry?
- How are your relationships with vendors and strategic partners?
- What challenges do your competitors pose?
- Are you struggling to find your target clientele, the best vendors, and the right employees?

Take a few minutes to list your biggest roadblocks. List these challenges on the left side of the page under the heading, "Challenges." Knowing your adversary is crucial to winning the battle.

Now, take the next few minutes to explain how your business will transform for the better when you overcome these challenges.

• What will your business look like when you overcome the challenges you described?

• How much more revenue and/or profit will you produce?

• What will this mean for your family, your company, your employees, and the important people in your life?

List the transformations and positive effects next to each challenge.

CHAPTER 7

The Benefit of Credibility
with Braun Mincher of PCG Telecom

In business, if you are not credible, you have nothing to stand on. We already talked about how traditional advertising is just a company tooting its own horn, which brings no credibility. When somebody else talks about you, it is much different. Think about a company you were considering using, and then explain what happened the minute you found out your friend used them too and was thrilled with their service. Winning an award is like receiving a monstrous referral! It is a trustworthy organization giving its stamp of approval.

In 2010, M & E was named a finalist for the national *Inc. Magazine* and *Winning Workplaces Top Small Workplaces Award*. In 2011, we were named a winner of the same award! I was recently at an appointment with a customer who values these organizations. He mentioned that as a result of knowing about these awards he wouldn't think twice about doing business with me. Not only did I stand out from the competition, but I also had the benefit of instant credibility due to this award. These factors won this customer over. Remember, winning one award like this is more valuable than years of self-promotion, or spending thousands of dollars on advertising.

Winning awards will not only make you more credible to customers, vendors, and team members, but many of the CEOs and entrepreneurs interviewed have mentioned the social credibility that also comes with these accolades. Obviously, there are great benefits to winning more jobs, attracting better talent, and having amazing relations with vendors, but social credibility in the entrepreneurial community is valuable as well.

It was a pleasure to sit down with Braun Mincher of PCG Telecom. He is the ultimate example of building credibility by winning awards. Braun has a long list of accomplishments in business and life, and I am honored to call him a friend. Braun and I sat down for coffee to talk about his experience with winning awards, and this is what he had to say.

Top of the Town in No Time
Braun Mincher: CEO, PCG Telecom
Fort Collins, CO
www.pcgtelecom.com

Matt Shoup: *Braun, what have been some of the biggest benefits you have seen from winning awards for yourself and your business?*

Braun Mincher: *The biggest thing these awards have done for me is to launch me, my name, and my credibility at a very young age into the business community. I feel like I got in and started applying at just the right time. I was an 18-year-old kid running Western Starr Charters and had to employ a base of people who were often twice my age. People wanted to work with a winner, and winning these awards gave me needed credibility at that age. I was also able to connect and build relationships with some of the state's and country's top entrepreneurs. Lastly, the media exposure I received was phenomenal.*

MS: *Tell me a little more about the credibility factor and how that may have tied in with media exposure and connecting with other entrepreneurs.*

BM: *One of the coolest things that the 1994* **Ernst and Young / Inc. Magazine Entrepreneur of the Year Award** *did was land me on the* **Today Show.** *Seven million people view this show daily, and I was instantly exposed to the nation as a credible and highly successful entrepreneur. Over 18 years later, we still leverage this appearance in our PR and marketing materials (plus the video is still available online for the world to see or Google search)! That is some big exposure showing my credibility, not to mention big media! These awards also allowed me to get my foot in the door when I wrote my book. As I put my book out there, and spoke with it, many people saw my awards and accolades, which proved my credibility. It gave me a good platform, with lots of options and opportunities.*

Being an award-winning entrepreneur allowed me to attain some big media and press while promoting my book, which then landed it as an award-winning book. One of the other big things was that I was introduced to, and able to spend time with other amazing entrepreneurs. I remember being 21-years-old and being able to spend time with and get to know people like Jake Jabs of American Furniture Warehouse. It has helped me immensely to get and stay connected.

MS: *Wow! This is all really amazing stuff. Let's talk a little more about the media exposure awards have brought you.*

BM: *I am a big believer that all media is good media. These awards, other than landing me on the* **Today Show,** *have landed me on other media venues as well. Another big one I did numerous* time was Neil Cavuto's national TV show. On top of that, local and regional newspapers, magazines, and television shows have had me make appearances and referred to me as an industry expert. I see each opportunity as another chance to expose myself to the public and build my credibility. The media exposure I received early on helped to launch me into the big leagues of the business world. The biggest thing about this media exposure is that I did not pay a penny for it!

MS: *That was one of my upcoming questions, so let's cover it now. How much time did you invest in applying for awards, and how much media exposure in dollars and cents did this get you? Let's use the* **Ernst and Young/ Inc. Magazine Entrepreneur of the Year Award** *as an example.*

BM: *I would say the amount of time I spent over two years to be named finalist and then winner of that award was four to ten hours. I would have paid easily over $100,000 to hire a PR firm to gain this media exposure if I hadn't won the award. I also think the ability to be viewed by over seven million people is priceless. Even at a penny per view, that is $70,000. It is by far the best marketing investment a business could make—getting free exposure from awards.*

MS: *You mentioned that when you wrote your book, you also leveraged and used these awards to promote yourself. Tell me about this.*

BM: *Yes, absolutely. Being an award-winning entrepreneur gave me immense credibility to talk about money and business in my book. I was able to re-engage many of the contacts I made earlier* in my 20s to help me with my book in terms of promotion and sales. This made it a lot easier than if I would have engaged in this venture without these accolades and connections.

MS: *What advice would you give to people who would like to make their businesses award-winning companies?*

BM: *Apply for as many awards as you can to get that experience. Realize that you will not win them all the time on the first try, but keep trying. Getting your name and face out there into the business and entrepreneurial community is a great thing. There is no such thing as bad PR.*

WORKING IT OUT

• What are you doing now to build credibility with your customers, vendors, potential team members, and the entrepreneurial community at large?
• How would this process be magnified and sped up as a result of winning awards?
• Think about vendors, potential team members, investors, banks, etc., and the credibility awards would give you with each.

- How do your sales presentation, marketing, and website alter as a result?
- How else would this overall credibility help to grow your company?
- Is there anything in your company right now that makes you lack credibility?
- If so, what do you need to do about it specifically, and by when?

CHAPTER 8

The Benefit of Local to International Exposure with Tonya Fitzpatrick of World Footprints Media

When a company wins an award, the organization giving the award releases this information to the press, media, and other news sources. Being a recipient of an award gives you exposure to an entirely new group of people and you do nothing and pay nothing to be connected to these people.

If you are planning to expand your business into new markets or territories (and even in you are not), news of your accomplishments may precede you. PR builds customer confidence in your company when they are being repeatedly and positively exposed to your name and brand. This news of your company will travel with the speed of the Internet, outside your office walls, your sphere of influence, and your geographic market. In addition to gaining more name and brand recognition inside and outside of your market, awards will open doors to connect you to people that will help you grow your business. Because most awards are posted online, they will also increase your SEO rankings, and exposure online.

I have made some amazing and profitable relationships with other people and companies worldwide as a result of this free exposure. When M & E was named as a finalist for a national award in *Inc. Magazine*, the owner of another painting company on the east coast contacted me. He and I began talking, and before I knew it, I was doing consulting work for his business. I cannot see any way I could have connected with him if it weren't for the exposure that being named as a finalist for this award provided. We've also received attention from bloggers eager to reference us on their blogs, giving us even more exposure.

The big point is that you never know where this news will end up. You never know who may click on a link, pick up a magazine, or open up a newspaper to see your award and your story. This initial contact can be the beginning of long-lasting business relationships.

In the next interview, Tonya Fitzpatrick with World Footprints Media shared with me how winning awards put her and her company on the international map. It was a lot of fun to talk with Tonya about her company and her award-winning radio show. Here is what we talked about.

Big Awards Attract Big Names and International Exposure
Tonya Fitzpatrick: CEO, World Footprints Media
Silver Spring, MD
www.worldfootprints.com

Matt Shoup: *Tonya, thanks for taking the time to allow me to interview you for this book. Tell me a little about what you do and how awards have come into play in your business.*

Tonya Fitzpatrick: *World Footprints is a multimedia company that has been in business since 2005. We produce the award-winning World Footprints radio show—a leading voice in* socially conscious and responsible travel and lifestyle. We talk about and focus on such subjects as fighting human trafficking, cultural heritage, history, voluntourism, and the environment, among others. We also focus on experiential travel and public diplomacy. As travelers, we carry the badge of "ambassador," and, thus, we seek to foster global citizenship through our broadcasts. Our programming is eclectic, entertaining, and informative, and listeners and website visitors will find us covering anything from a dinosaur dig to White House events.

One of the things that we are proud of is that we have big names who we have interviewed, and who support our cause. Being an award-winning broadcast organization has played a huge role in our being able to lock down some of these names, has given us credibility in our community, and has allowed us to use these awards to market and advertise in our community and world.

MS: *That's really amazing! So when did awards come into play for you?*

TF: *In 2010, we were in Vancouver during the Olympics, and during the last week of the games, we received notification that we had been awarded the top travel broadcast distinction. This award set us apart from other "general" travel media broadcasts; this was huge for us because of the show we submitted for consideration. Our show was called "**On the Road to Freedom**," and it was a historical broadcast that included interviews with authors and people who explored the civil rights movement. The great thing about this award was that it was judged by an esteemed panel of industry judges, and the winner was selected from an international pool. There were radio shows in the United Kingdom, Canada, and Mexico that were competing with us, and* it was such an honor to be named the winner of this award (**Best Travel Broadcast, 2009, North American Association Travel Journalists Association**).

We have also been nominated for a distinguished Lowell Thomas Award, and a couple of destination awards.

MS: *Tell me about the exposure and what it did for your show.*

TF: *This award immediately got our name out there in the international community and gave us a lot of recognition. One of the big things that happened is that the award has made it easier to go after interviews with like-minded celebrities and news-makers. We are certainly seen as a more credible organization, so in addition to the high-profile interviews, we are also granted access to cover many high-profile events. I think that, without this award, our achievements, exposure, and access would have been harder to accomplish.*

The other big thing is that, in some industries, some awards are purchased or not prestigious to achieve. The award we won was a highly credible one in our industry and is not one that just anybody can go and get. It was granted from a valid and recognized association. This award told us that the community recognized what we were doing as travel journalists.

MS: *What kind of time have you spent applying for awards, and what kind of return on investment have you seen?*

TF: *We only spent about three or four hours applying for these awards. For us, it is hard to put a monetary value on what these awards have brought. The biggest return is a strong and positive brand and awareness of our show and organization. We* definitely know that some of the interviews we have locked down are due to the award, and other nominations. Lastly, the award has really helped to build momentum and launch us forward into the public eye.

MS: *What advice would you give to entrepreneurs looking to win awards?*

TF: *Be sure to do research on awards, and make sure the organizations offering the awards are credible. If you apply for and win an award that is not credible, it may hurt you more than help you. Be sure to do your due diligence.*

CHAPTER 9

The Benefit of Free Press and Media Exposure with Greg Jenkins of Bravo Productions

One of the biggest benefits I have seen from winning awards has been all the FREE press you get when you win. When I won the *Top Young Professional Award* from *ColoradoBiz Magazine*, the magazine arranged a photo shoot. They put my picture on the cover of an issue that was distributed to over 60,000 business owners in Colorado. I can't even count how many painting, consulting, and speaking deals I received because of this cover. To advertise on a full page inside a magazine like this would have cost $6,780 (wonder how much the cover would cost if they allowed it?), but I received this press for free. When you start winning awards, a lot of press of this nature will come with virtually no effort on your part.

Yet, with a little bit of extra effort, you can multiply this press. When you win an award, you can easily create your own press release to send it to your media contacts. You can also call them and ask them to note your achievement, or pitch the story of your award to a writer as an entire piece. If you do not have any media contacts, an easy place to start is with your local newspapers or magazines. Most newspapers have an "applause" section perfect for this. When you introduce yourself, let them know you have a great story for them. As you begin to meet writers and editors, they will look to you in the future as a trusted source of valuable business information. Your credibility and accolades may encourage them to contact you for helping them with other stories about local business as well. These contacts will produce profit and exposure over the years, so be sure to build and update this list.

Free press and media have counted for tens to hundreds of thousands of dollars of exposure for my company. I was able to meet with Greg Jenkins of Bravo Productions to hear about how awards have brought exposure to his company, worth about $1 million. Greg's energy was contagious as we spoke on the phone, and he truly has an amazing company. Check out what he has to say about winning awards.

A Million Dollars' Worth of Exposure
Greg Jenkins: CEO, Bravo Productions
Long Beach, CA
www.bravo-eventsonline.com

Matt Shoup: *Greg, you have a very impressive story and company. Can you tell me a little about your business and how awards have come into play?*

Greg Jenkins: *Thanks, Matt. Out of college, before I helped to found Bravo, I worked in corporate ad agencies. This work taught me a lot, but I was an entrepreneur at heart, and knew I was going to kill myself with the crazy corporate hours, so I decided to found Bravo in 1987. The company has had some transitions through the years, but awards have played a major role in our growth, credibility, and separation from the competition. It has also helped us directly to close business we may have never closed.*

MS: *Great! I am looking forward to digging into this. Tell me about some of the awards, and please also explain to the reader who may not be familiar with your industry the importance of these awards.*

GJ: *I'm glad you asked that. Many of our awards are industry specific and not well known. For example, we have been nominated numerous times for and have won a* **Gala Award**. *Many outsiders would see this award and not know the significance of it.*

MS: *Exactly, I have no idea how important this award is. Can you tell me more?*

GJ: *This award is like winning an Oscar in our industry. This is an award that many peers worldwide will never be nominated for, let alone win. It was a prestigious honor for us to receive it, and it has skyrocketed our credibility.*

MS: *Tell me about some other awards that may be industry specific.*

GJ: *We have also won an* **Esprit Award**, *which equates to winning a* **Golden Globe** *in our industry. The cool thing about this award is that the judges do not know which companies they are judging until they select the winner! We were very honored and happy to win this award too.*

MS: *Many entrepreneurs I have interviewed have talked about credibility from awards. Tell me more about this.*

GJ: *Absolutely. Credibility is one of the biggest things we have received from awards. Going hand in hand with that is the* international exposure we have received. The first example is that we won an award, which a colleague in Mexico subsequently read about, and then contacted us to do business together. Obviously that exposure was one benefit, but they decided to contact us because of the credibility that the award brought us. Another was a company that we interviewed for a book we were writing. As we got to talking, they asked us to do some work for them in the Caribbean. Again, the same thing rings true here. Thanks to the awards, we were past the point of needing to prove we were credible, which can be a huge obstacle and task for a company that does not win awards. The credibility is great to have within the industry, to show that we are one of the best at what we do. But the big money-maker is our clients already having the confidence in us before we even start working together. Once we do start working together, it reinforces what they already think.

MS: *Tell me more about your industry and how awards separate you from competitors?*

GJ: *This industry is a lot like yours, I am sure. There are no regulations, no licenses, and no policing to make sure that things are being done to any standards. Anybody can go print a business card and say that they do what we do!*

MS: *Amen to that!*

GJ: *But, the big difference is that we will always out-perform the companies that are winging it because we are an award-winning company. This separates us from others that are not. For example, a realtor needs a license, and a lawyer needs to pass the bar, so there is a standard that is expected when anybody goes to* do business with these professionals. In my industry, there is a large discrepancy between what we do, what other "professional" companies do, and then what the other guys do.

Being an award-winning company gives us the credibility and separation for our clients to know that, although there are no standards, our industry has recognized us as one of the best! This gives comfort, security, and peace of mind to clients.

One of the other things this does is attract key leaders and employees to the company, and morale is boosted in our office. It also retains key team members. Any entrepreneur knows that one of the biggest costs is employee replacement and retraining. If we can keep our key people around for a long time, it keeps our work consistent, which adds to our credibility. It also lets our vendors know that we are a dependable company they can rely on.

MS: *You have obviously received some great free exposure from these awards. How much do you think (in terms of dollars and cents) you have received?*

GJ: *Matt, to be completely honest with you, I was thinking about this last week when I knew I was planning on talking with you. I figured we have received close to $1 million in free exposure!*

MS: *Are you serious?*

GJ: *Yes, absolutely. Here are a few examples. When we won one award, the **Los Angeles Business Journal** did a free two-page spread on us. That ad would have easily cost $20,000 if we had advertised with them, and we got it for free. Even if we back out the investment of the little time we spent to win the award, it was free!*

Another example is that the news does a story on us during the prime time 5:00pm news hour. These segments are repeated and shown many times on multiple stations. They are like little 30-second commercials and they hold more relevance in my eyes because they are not actually commercials—just the news reporting facts. You can easily rack up $100,000 in exposure with one or two awards. I feel that any entrepreneur on any budget cannot afford not to do this! It is a must.

MS: *That is amazing. Thanks for sharing that. Can you tell me what advice you would give to entrepreneurs and business owners looking to follow in the footsteps of award-winning companies?*

GJ: *Sure. I would say that the biggest obstacle I think a lot of companies face is that inner voice in their head that says, "I am not good enough, and nobody would give me an award." Kick that voice out of your head permanently. Remember that what you think and believe will very much manifest in your life and business, so get your mind aligned with success, and know you can compete with these award-winning companies. Remember that every award-winning company had a time when they applied for and won their first award, and I bet that they had the same fears and thoughts that any reader might.*

Remember that you have to put in the work to apply and sell your story to win these awards. They don't just fall out of the sky. Once you start applying, the entries will get better, and your story will become more and more refined. Think of your application as a chance to tell your story, and remember that everybody has a great story. Also remember that as much as you would like to share your story, there are just as many people that want to hear it.

Finally, practice, practice, practice. Over time, your ratio of awards won vs. awards applied for will rise. Just remember, your story is amazing and wonderful, and you must first believe it, then pitch it in a way that the judges just can't put it down. Don't worry about that first rejection letter you get. Don't give up, and remember that you are not going to win them all. Start locally and build momentum, but don't restrict yourself from thinking nationally and globally. Remember that this is one of the best things you can do for your business.

WORKING IT OUT

If you haven't done so already, make a list of all your contacts and connections in the media world.
This list should include writers, editors, owners, and operators of publications.

Send them an introduction card. That's right, a real card in the real mail, not an email, or a call just yet.

(See Appendix II for a great card-sending resource!)

Mention that you will be calling them soon to try to set up a time to get coffee and share your story with them. To sweeten the deal, include a $5 gift card to a local coffee shop.

Use these examples as a springboard for creating an attention-grabbing script:

#1

Thank you for allowing me to introduce myself to you. I follow your work in The Post and enjoy what I read. I'd love to be able to provide you with some awesome stories, and would appreciate the chance to share my business with you. I'll call next week to see when you have time for a quick coffee, on me. Looking forward to putting a face to the name!

#2

I just read your story about economy-boosting practices in the ABC Town Times on Monday. I am excited to share a story that would piggyback on that article. As I am connected with a large network of local businessmen and women, I would also love to create a working relationship so as to be a viable source of business news in the community. I will call you next week to see if there might be time for us to connect over coffee, on me!

A week later, make the calls to invite those people to sit down. Does it encourage you to know that I have never been rejected for a sit-down when I sent a nice card with a $5 coffee gift card? It's true, so take heart! It is a great lead-in. Here are a script and some pointers for getting an appointment:

You: *Is Tom there?*
Tom: *This is Tom.*
You: *Tom, Hi! This is Matt with M & E Painting. I just wanted to follow-up and make sure you received my card.*
Tom: *Matt, I sure did. Thank you so much. What's up?*
You: *I know you're busy. Is this a good time? (This is crucial as media people are on deadlines.)*
Tom: *Sure, I have a quick minute.*
You: *Great, I will be brief. Tom, as I mentioned in the card, I would love to buy you coffee and sit down with you to tell you a little about my company and make sure I can be a lead source for you when you need me. When are you free for 30 minutes to meet in the next few weeks?*

Here they will give you a yes or a no, or they might ask for you to call back.

Most of the time they will not say no. The media always wants to be connected to potential stories. If they say yes, set up a time, and call the day prior to your appointment to confirm. Make sure to respect their time by being on time yourself. If they ask to be called back, set a time to do this and follow up accordingly until you get your meeting.

When you sit down, make sure to share your story.

(You should have worked on this by now.) Usually, the story that appeals to an awards panel of judges will also appeal to the media people you talk to. Remember, these people will be a very valuable asset to your company, but their time is also valuable and deadline driven. Be sure to give them what they need in a short amount of time. For now, just concentrate on making your list.

Once you get your list, you can send your cards and do your follow-ups. Make sure to finish reading this book and working through the Working It Out exercises, or the accompanying workbook before you call the media. Practice a few rounds of scripts with another company member or trusted colleague. Have fun, and have them hit you from different angles with responses.

I have cold called, sent letters, emailed, door-knocked, and dropped by, but I have never had more success in turning a potential lead into an actual meeting than with sending a card in the mail with a personal message and a $5 coffee card. Do this, and you, too, will have results.

CHAPTER 10

The Benefit of Closing More Sales with Tami Spaulding of The Group, Inc. Real Estate

Being an award-winning company will ultimately lead you to more sales. Credibility and standing out from your competition, combined with greater exposure in the media and general public, is a recipe for explosive sales growth. Sales are obviously more than just going into an appointment and bragging to your potential customer about yourself and your company. Your goal in a sales situation should be to deliver take-away value for your customers.

The old saying is true: They must first know you, then like you, then trust you before they buy from you. When you enter a sales situation with awards to your name, you are allowing them to know you, because your name has already been out in public, and trust you because an entity they trust has bestowed an award on you. As soon as I started winning awards, I immediately noticed that people knew my company. I entered sales appointments, and there was not as much ice to break.

I recently met with the owners of a local company we do business with. As one of them entered the room, he stopped and said, "Hey, I know you! You were on the cover of *ColoradoBiz Magazine* last year. I read the article, nice work!" He was immediately comfortable with me because he felt he already knew me.

On another occasion, during an estimate, the customer pulled out a local newspaper that mentioned our recent placement on the 2010 *Inc. 5000 List*. The customer was himself a business owner and mentioned that he understood what this type of award means about a company. He noted that none of the other local painters were close to our caliber, and immediately signed with us. I didn't even have to work at closing the deal; the customer did it for me!

As I mentioned earlier, Simon Sinek says in his book, *Start with Why*, that "people don't buy what you do, they buy why you do it."

I recently asked a customer what was important to him when hiring a painter. He mentioned that he really loves people that are on time. I dug a little deeper to find that the last contractor he worked with showed up late to discuss the job. The customer left the work site and sped over to his son's baseball game, already in progress. He arrived late, and missed his son making a huge play in the second inning. His son had looked for his dad in the stands, but did not find him there. So, for this customer, being on time was the "what." His "why" was about keeping commitments with his kids. He was looking for a contractor to respect his time so he could spend more of it with his son.

Finding out such concerns and addressing them will make you a sales superstar. Listen closely to your customer. When you hear the what, go deeper. Discover the why that motivates the what. The many whats of life can easily be dismissed for others, but the why will remain and people will gladly pay money to ensure that their whys are respected. This simple technique shows customers that you are listening to their needs. It also clearly proves that you are more than just a company offering them a service; you are connecting with them on a human level.

Tami Spaulding is the master at closing business because of the way she works with her customers. Her deep understanding of their whys is what has made her so successful. Actually, I met Tami when I was 10 years old (and she has the buck-toothed pictures of me to prove it, but they are under lock and key). She sold my parents their house when we moved from New Jersey to Colorado in the early 90s. By then she had already been named an award-winning realtor, and to this date holds a deep-rooted reputation in the Northern Colorado community. Here is what Tami had to share about her experiences winning awards.

In a Soft Way, Be Known
Tami Spaulding: Realtor, The Group, Inc. Real Estate
Fort Collins, CO
www.talk2tami.com

Matt Shoup: *Tell me a little about you, your career as a realtor, and how awards have come into play.*

Tami Spaulding: *I got started as a realtor in 1987, after working in the title business for a number of years. My philosophy has always been that it's not about me—it's about what I can do for others. I always keep this in mind when working with my clients. Over the years, I have had thousands of transactions with clients, and my goal is to always make each one feel that they are the only client I have. I was honored to be named **Rookie of the Year Realtor** in 1987, by the Fort Collins Board of Realtors. That was huge exposure for me, as it gave buyers and sellers confidence in me as a new and fresh realtor.*

MS: *Tell me a little more about this. I am sure a "rookie" realtor has many obstacles to overcome.*

TS: *Definitely. When I began, I was young, and people didn't know me, so my goal for the year was to be the best and make myself known. Winning this award immediately gave me credibility and said, "Hey, Tami is here to stay and make a big positive impact in the real estate world." Again, I always focused on serving my customers; doing this well, and having solid sales figures helped me to lock down this award. I remember there were a lot of people who saw that I won the award, and more than the credibility was the exposure. This was huge in building peer and customer recognition, and was a big confidence booster for me. It also confirmed that I deserved all the benefits of the hard work I was putting in. It gave me something I could market to the public.*

MS: *You mentioned the exposure was huge. Tell me more about this.*

TS: *I am not 100% sure that anybody saw that I was the **Rookie of the Year**, and then did business with me, but I do know that I received a lot of exposure. It seemed like everywhere I went, people were mentioning this award, and giving me congratulations and praise. Just the idea of my name being out in the realtor and client community was extremely important for a young up-and-coming realtor at the time.*

MS: *Tell me more about the confidence that this award gave you.*

TS: *As I mentioned, **Rookie of the Year** was an important goal* *for me in my first year. You only have one chance to get it, and they only name one. The confidence boost was huge. I always go into business situations with the mind-set to win and that I am going to do the best job for my customer. I had confidence before the award, but the award just increased it.*

MS: *Tell me a little more about your style of marketing and letting others know about your awards. How do you leverage them?*

TS: *I always feel that if you take care of the customer and do what is right for them, the rest will come. For me the rest is just icing on the cake. I am very subtle about the way I present my awards. I want my customers to know that they are going with me because of the extreme confidence they have in me, and for my reputation of taking care of customers. My advice is to be known as an award-winner in a soft way. During a listing presentation, or when I meet with buyers, I hand them a packet that tells them a little about me. There is a page that mentions the awards. I do not go on and on about it. I want people to say, "I see why she is an award winner," based on my actions and service to them. I do not ever like to brag or show off the awards. There is a fine art of being subtly known, and I feel that companies that do that will come out ahead.*

MS: *You have said that some of the awards you have won fell into your lap. One of the myths I talk about states that this is not how it happens. Can you speak to this?*

TS: *In the real estate industry, things are a little different than the norm in terms of awards. They actually do go out and search for people to give these awards to, so this myth is actually true in* my industry. I am sure that in many others, such as yours, and the majority of your readers', it is a myth. Entrepreneurs still need to go out and find awards to apply for and take action!

MS: *What other kinds of advice do you have for entrepreneurs reading this book in terms of how you have used and leveraged your awards?*

TS: *No matter what awards you have, never let the customers see dollar signs in your eyes. The advice I always give about this business is to make each customer feel they are your only customer when you are with them. Also, be very careful about not relying on the award to give you success. As I mentioned, this is just icing on the cake. You cannot forget about the basics of business and being great for the clients you serve.*

MS: *Tami, this has been great. What advice would you give to entrepreneurs attempting to win their first awards?*

TS: *Go out and research. Search and find the criteria for the awards. Make winning these awards written goals you have for yourself, and then work at being able to meet the criteria to the best of your ability. Another big piece of advice is to always give the awards people 110%; give them more than what they want. Always do more than they are looking for, as you never know what that little thing will be that may sway them toward choosing you. And of course, in a soft way, be known.*

Working It Out

- Think of your sales process, from initial contact to the closed deal and beyond. Where could you use the ammunition of being an award-winning company to win more sales?
- Create a list of each step your company has within its sales process. Next to each item, explain how this step of the sales process could be improved by the addition of awards won.
- Where can you add extra value, build more of the "know, like, and buy" cycle to this process?
- From the previous section, how are you different from your competitors, and how do you show this value to customers?
- How much do you think your sales could increase based on this strategy? Put it in terms of dollars and cents.
- Are there tie-ups or snags in your sales process that will be relieved?
- If you have a sales team, how will you be able to implement this into your sales training?

CHAPTER 11

The Benefit of Recruiting and Maintaining a High Caliber Team with Jodie Shaw of ActionCOACH United States

Being an award-winning company is just part of the development and creation of an ever-evolving company culture. Culture is extremely important to every business, and the owner is in the driver's seat of determining, defining, creating, and molding this culture. This also rings true when it comes to recruiting and retaining a high caliber team. Bringing people into the organization that mold and fit with your culture is extremely important, and you will feel it when you have a good fit, just as you will when you don't.

Let's say the best painter in the country moves to Northern Colorado, and needs to find a job. He will probably go to the Internet and begin to search for "painters." As he surfs, our name will be the one that just keeps popping up and as he scrolls through our website, the multiple logos noting our awards will most certainly put us at the top of his list. When he comes into the office for an interview, he will see our lobby covered with certificates, awards, and plaques. What will he think about us compared to the last painter's office?

Like any notoriety, winning awards brings a level of accountability. An award-winning company is expected to be great, and I love living up to that expectation. I agree with

Braun Mincher's comment, "People want to work for a winner and a winning company."

Back to this job-seeking painter: When he begins to work for M & E Painting, and becomes a part of our continued success, we demonstrate to him that we are indeed a top small workplace, the fastest growing, the most innovative, and that the CEO is a top young professional. What does this do to his long-term confidence in his job security? How does it affect his dedication to work hard every day? What does this kind of team member say to a customer? What do you think your customers will think and say about you, knowing you attracted the top talent in the country to your company? And, your new team member knows he needs to give his all to your company everyday, because there are probably ten more talented applicants hoping to take his place.

Being an award-winning company allows you to hire not just anyone that comes along, but to recruit the best and the brightest. Besides the benefit of pay, you will be able to show a potential team member the benefits of working for a company seen as a leader in the industry. This is just like the process of selling to a customer. Recruiting is selling yourself to possible employees. Many times, employers think hiring is a one-way street, but, "Why should I hire you?" is not the only question to consider. Business owners who know this always have the most loyal and profitable team members. If you are not considering that you need to share your company's story, history, mission, and vision to prove why someone should come and work for you, then you shouldn't be surprised by a high turnover rate. Recruiting is very intentional and makes for longer lasting and more loyal team members. Hiring to fill seats is a dead end road.

Since we began winning awards, amazing people who want to work for us have contacted us. Because of that, we have been able to raise the standard of what we look for in team members and avoid people who don't fit with our values and culture. It costs a great deal of time, effort, and money to hire and train for any position you are looking to fill. Being sure to do it right the first time is a huge part of low turnover that allows you to spend your business dollars on better things. Being an award-winning company will help you be more profitable and efficient in this department as well.

The next interview explains this concept and benefit extremely well. Jodie Shaw and I spent some time on the phone, and it was a pleasure to talk with her. She is the CEO of ActionCOACH United States and Canada, and she shared with me what award winning has done for the company, and also how it has tested and proven their leadership. Here is what Jodie had to share.

A Litmus Test of Our Leadership
Jodie Shaw: CEO, ActionCOACH,
United States and Canada
Las Vegas, NV
www.actioncoach.com

Matt Shoup: *Tell me a little about ActionCOACH, your role, and how winning awards has impacted the company.*

Jodie Shaw: *ActionCOACH is a global franchise that coaches entrepreneurs to reach their goals and grow their companies. We are different in the industry because we offer a money-back guarantee. We promise to show a measurable return on investment to our* clients: for every dollar they spend on our coaching they will receive a return. We have over 1,000 coaches worldwide that range from single at-home office coaches to franchisees that are building firms with multiple employed coaches. We are in 39 countries around the world, and we are opening in three to four new markets per year. Our typical franchisee coach coaches about 15 business owners one-on-one per year.

We have won over 100 awards over the life of our company, and have even created our own awards, one for our coaches and one for businesses! The award we created for our coaches goes annually to the franchisee that has the most award-winning clients. One of our franchisee goals is to help their customers, who are other entrepreneurs and business owners, win awards for their companies. Our coaches play a behind-the-scenes role to help them with this.

MS: Wow! Tell me more about the award you created.

JS: We see the power and value of awards in a business, so every year we have all of our franchisees report the number of awards that each of their clients have received for their individual business. We then give an award to the franchisee whose clients have the most awards. The coaches play such a big behind-the-scenes role with their clients in winning awards, so it is great to corporately recognize them for their hard work.

MS: Jodie, what have been some of the benefits you have seen for ActionCOACH from winning awards?

JS: The obvious goal of ActionCOACH as franchisor is to attract and connect with people wanting to become entrepreneurs and buy into our business model. Before they even talk to us, we estimate they will do about 12 hours of research. Much of this will be on the Internet. Being an award-winning company builds our credibility as a brand and as a company of merit.

One of the awards (it may be better to call it a ranking) we receive is from the **Franchise Business Review**. An independent organization interviews our franchisees to see how they feel about us as the franchisor. They ask questions regarding support, morale, systems, and how we support and ensure franchisee success. This report is a litmus test of the leadership of the company, and I love seeing the rankings every year. We always place high, and this is great to use in our marketing, PR, and advertising to new prospective franchisees.

Having this credibility as a company to show to the public, our potential clients, and our potential franchisees continues to drive our success. There are many other coaching franchises that do not have this credibility, and I know this is what separates us.

MS: *What have been some of the most memorable or meaningful awards for ActionCOACH and why?*

JS: *As I mentioned, the* **Franchise Business Review** *is an excellent one. Another recent one was the* **Stevie Awards**. *We won* **Best Overall Company**! *It was an honor for us because the other businesses competing for that award also had amazing stories and were prominent across the country.*

Another really cool one we won was actually a marketing video. We created a video called "I Am an ActionCOACH," and it was a marketing tool designed to show potential franchisees what we do. We never made the video with any intentions to win an award for it. We did, however, win a **Hermes Award** for this video! This was amazing because we were going up against ad agencies that are doing this all day, every day, and for our internal marketing team to win this award really spoke to the dedication and skill of the team. It showed that we could compete with huge ad agencies.

MS: These are some really big awards! What other benefits have you seen?

JS: A large benefit was the boost to team and company morale. Knowing that we are the best of the best really boosts the atmosphere and helps add to the culture and positive environment of the company. It is important to us that our employees understand we are a global leader that strives to raise the bar year after year. When we won a lot of our awards, it was in an economy in which there was a lot of doom, gloom, and bad news out there, especially when it came to being a business owner. Winning these awards helped us to fly above all that noise.

Another benefit is all the PR and media exposure you receive. When these awards are won, there are always press releases and stories written about the company. It also helps with your SEO rankings as your company name and website are bow-tied to these prestigious websites, which helps you move up in the ranks of Google.

These awards can also be leveraged in all of our marketing efforts. Marketing material that goes out to potential franchisees always mentions our awards and Franchise Business Report rankings. For our franchisees to know that they are a part of an award-winning franchisor is also important, as they can leverage this when they go out to win clients.

The other big thing that awards do is to continue to show

to our franchisees that we are a forward moving and thinking company, and that we are always striving to stay fresh and innovative. We have a long-term relationship and investment with our franchisees. Their success ultimately means our success, and that is important to us.

MS: *What advice would you give to entrepreneurs looking to win awards?*

JS: *Look for what the judges are looking for, and when you apply, remember that the judges are reading your entry. Spend quality time on the awards package and make sure it is presented professionally. Whether you or your marketing department do this, make sure it gets done correctly. Invest in a quality editor or copywriter, and be sure that you are selling your company and being persuasive in your submissions. Judges want to be sold and have a reason to keep your story at the top of the pile.*

A big thing we do is to keep a massive awards calendar with all awards deadlines and reminders three weeks out. We are always updating this calendar with new awards we wish to apply for. Also, join mailing lists to make sure that you are kept in the loop for new awards. Be on the constant lookout for awards.

WORKING IT OUT

- Think of your current company culture. What would becoming an award-winning company do for your company culture?

- How would it affect your recruiting process?

- What does your recruiting process look like?
- Do recruits know your vision? What is their vision?
- How do you find out what is most important in a career with potential team members?
- What does your interview process look like?
- Do you feel like you are truly recruiting, or are you merely hiring and filling seats?
- How would this change if you were an award-winning company?
- Once you begin to win awards, how will this change the standard of your company, and what you look for in a team member?
- Do you feel that you will be able to attract and retain better talent?
- What will this do for your productivity, profitability, and efficiency?

CHAPTER 12

The Benefit of a Morale Boost
with Cammie Cable of CLEARLINK

As I mentioned before, company culture is a huge part of any business, and team morale fits right into culture. How is morale in your company right now? Imagine your company winning a prestigious business award and the benefit it will bring to the team. Especially in today's business landscape, many employees are fearful of the possibility of losing their job due to market instability. With big corporate layoffs, downsizing, and the flagrant disregard for the welfare of employees, imagine the morale boost when your company wins an award that fixes you in the industry as a leading, fastest growing, or top workplace. As your company is mentioned in the media and the family and friends of your employees mention how great it is that they work for an award-winning company, what do you think that does to the morale of your employees?

Being an award-winning company not only boosts morale, but also raises the standard of what is expected from a work team. As higher caliber people enter your organization, this improvement will also boost morale and culture.

When M & E Painting won the *Inc. Magazine* and *Winning Workplaces Award* in 2011, we held a celebration BBQ. The anticipation leading up to it was mentioned by many of the team members in meetings, at the office, on job sites, and during social gatherings. As we wrapped up the celebration, we all circled around in the back of our office and each M & E team member was given their own engraved M & E Painting shot glass. We all had a celebratory toast and took a shot to celebrate the award. You could feel the camaraderie in the air. As we have won more awards, the tone of the office feels more like a celebration every day.

I had the chance to speak with Cammie Cable of CLEARLINK. She described many of the benefits of the Utah-based company's extensive list of awards. The one point that kept coming up over and over had to do with morale, and the boost of morale for team members that comes from their company winning awards. Not only has CLEARLINK won tons of awards, but they also took on a challenge that I have never heard of a company doing before. They planned to set a world record together as a team; talk about a morale boost! Here is what Cammie had to say.

Not Just Award Winning, But World Record Setting
Cammie Cable: Director of Human Resources, CLEARLINK
Salt Lake City, UT
www.clearlink.com

Matt Shoup: *Cammie, please tell me a little about the growth of your company, and where and how awards have come into play.*

Cammie Cable: *We started as a small Utah company, have organically grown over the years, and have become firmly rooted in Utah and the community. One of the goals of our company is* to partner with national brands to help them expand their client bases. Winning awards for our company built excellent credibility and reliability, and these national companies know we will do a great job for them and be around for the long haul. When we made the **Inc. 5000 List** for growth, it showed these brands that we mean business, and gave them confidence we could build their companies. It showed them we have a steady brand (as they do), as well as our stability over time. It also helped us to acquire larger companies that we wanted to partner with.

MS: Tell me a little about what winning awards has done for the workplace.

CC: When we first started, we never recruited talent from out of state. Once we began winning awards and gaining more and more attention, we were contacted from top talent from across the country. We had people wanting to know what our company was all about and wanting to work with us. What appealed to many is we were growing in a down economy, which let them know that there would be stability for their position over the years.

MS: What other benefits have awards brought to your company?

CC: We want to hire and retain top talent, as we work in a high call center environment. Our partners and brands want to know that there is an environment and culture that values and takes care of its team members. Our investors want to know where we are going and that we have sustainability over time. Awards have done this for us, and have confirmed the amazing culture and environment we are trying to create.

MS: *I have heard that you are not only an award-wining company but also a* **Guinness Book of World Records** *record holding company!*

CC: *Yes, we are! As we began to win awards and saw the culture and team building that this created, we decided to set a world record together as a company. We live in Utah and are close to the snowy mountains. We organized a day, brought together many team members and their family members to the mountains, and we built 1,279 snowmen in one hour!*

MS: *Out of all the companies I interviewed, I have never interviewed a record setting one. What kind of impact did this have on CLEARLINK?*

CC: *It really brought the team together, and gave them the feeling that they were a part of something. For them to be able to say that they were part of setting a world record with their company was really something amazing. We had over 300 people do this together. Another thing we incorporated was donating money for each snowman built to* **Youth Making a Difference**. *This also brought us together with the community.*

MS: *That is remarkable, Cammie! No wonder you are an award-winning company. What advice would you give to entrepreneurs looking to win their first awards?*

CC: *One of the big things we considered was what we wanted CLEARLINK to portray and look like to our community. This process gave our company the opportunity to find out what we were internally, and express that culture to the community at large. It is* *a nice thing to know where you stand in the community. Another piece of advice is to get yourself out there. You may win, you may not, but you never know where this will lead.*

WORKING IT OUT

- Describe the morale of your workplace currently.
- Do you think it could be better?
- Do you need to let anybody go to improve this culture?
- If so, when will you do it? (I know this can be difficult, but trust me, you'll wish you had done it sooner.)
- What will happen to your company once you do this?
- What will winning awards do for your company's morale?
- What specific awards could you win that would be a significant morale booster?

CHAPTER 13

The Benefit of Leverage That Lasts Forever with Lee Prosenjak of Cherry Creek Dance

One of the really cool things about winning awards is that you can continue to leverage them for years after you win them. Because entrepreneurs love to leverage their money, people, and time, the idea of following seven simple steps to win an award that your company can capitalize on for life is appealing.

I have gotten to know Lee Prosenjak with Cherry Creek Dance over the years through our common membership in EO. Lee is a truly passionate entrepreneur and has grown an amazing company. His company has a long list of awards to its name, but the thing that hit home for me as we talked was how he has been able to leverage these awards year after year. Check out what Lee had to say about leveraging his company's awards.

Credibility and Leverage
That Lasts a Lifetime
Lee Prosenjak: CEO, Cherry Creek Dance
Denver, CO
www.cherrycreekdance.com

Matt Shoup: *Lee, you and Stephanie, your wife and co-owner of the studio, have accumulated a lot of awards over the past 12 years. Can you please speak on one or two that have been the most prominent and have had the most impact on your business?*

Lee Prosenjak: *In 1999, we were the proud recipients of an award from the Denver magazine, **5280**. They have an editor's and people's choice award for many different categories. We were named **Best Birthday Party** in Denver. At the time, we had one to two birthday parties per month, and the immediate result of this award was that we doubled our birthday party bookings. Another award we won was from **Colorado Parent Magazine**. For 10 of the past 12 years, that publication has offered a **Best of the Best Award**, and we have been named **Best of the Best** for dance studios in Denver. The benefit has been ongoing and consistent name recognition in our community. Parents are proud to send their kids to a school with those kinds of accolades, and proud to tell other parents about us. This award has also increased revenue and morale over the years.*

MS: *Talk more about the **5280** award and how you have leveraged it for your business, as well as any benefits you have seen in addition to increased revenue.*

LP: *It's funny you ask, because I was just thinking about this award the other day. When we won it, we had a plaque made to hang on* the wall in our lobby. I also received the rights to use the logo in our marketing and branding, and I have even included it in my email signature. Twelve years later, we still mention this award as one of our selling points. It still has the same value and "punch" that it did back then. We mention this award in everything we do, and it has become synonymous with Cherry Creek Dance.

MS: *It sounds like you do a great job of leveraging and promoting your awards. Can you speak to the entrepreneurs reading this book about how to do this and how often they should do it?*

LP: *Sure. It is up to you, the business owner, to take the award and leverage it for yourself. The initial award for us created its own buzz, and we saw a spike in birthday party revenue. After the initial buzz and promotion that comes with such an award, it is up to you to continue to push, promote, and leverage the award. The more you do this, the more beneficial it becomes. As I already mentioned, we have done this so much with the **5280** award that it has become synonymous with our name. You say, "Cherry Creek Dance," to anyone local, and they think, "amazing birthday party."*
Make sure you profit from the exponential benefit that awards will bring by using them to your advantage and promoting them actively. It's just like anything in business. There will always be passive customers that come to you, but an entrepreneur also needs to get up, go out, and proactively promote.

MS: *How about the **Colorado Parent Magazine** award? You seem to be the defending champion in Denver! Can you tell me about how this award has affected your business?*

LP: *This award has also helped us increase our revenue. One of the other cool things is that each year, when voting time comes, it develops and fosters camaraderie within the school. Parents frequently turn in their ballots, and mention the voting to others. We do a big push and promotion to our contacts to make sure they vote. This is met with positive feedback and response. We are proud to also have the selling point that we are consistently chosen as **Best of the Best**, especially knowing how many amazing dance schools there are in Denver.*

MS: *How many hours do you estimate you have spent over the past 12 years applying for and attempting to win awards, and what has the dollar amount been on the return?*

LP: *It has been very minimal, and maybe one of the least time-consuming things we do in our marketing. I would say somewhere around 40 hours total over the past 12 years, and would estimate about a $20,000 range of immediate benefit and exposure. The biggest thing it has done is skyrocket our credibility as one of the top dance schools in Denver, and that is hard to put a price tag on. That credibility is also one that will continue to grow and snowball, and once you have that award to your name, it cannot be taken away. That credibility sustains over time.*

MS: *What advice do you have for entrepreneurs reading this book who want to turn their businesses into award-winning companies?*

LP: *"Why not?" That's what I said, and then I saw the results. Winning awards has a low barrier to entry from a cost and time standpoint, yet the benefits are amazing. It gives you a way to build your credibility overnight and something to leverage for a* lifetime in your business. It will certainly make you break away from the pack. I spend a lot of time with other entrepreneurs from across the state and country, and have discovered that there are companies that win awards and those that don't. All the companies that do seem to be ahead of the game and above the competition. The PR and media exposure is wonderful! I highly recommend it to any entrepreneur.

CHAPTER 14

The Benefit of the Boost You May Need with Matt Butler of ROLLORS

Winning an award could be just the boost your company needs. The timing of the award could happen right as your business is about to make or break it. Some companies struggle to scale up and get their hobby turned into a full-time passion that pays the bills. I had the opportunity to talk to Matt Butler of ROLLORS. He designed, manufactured, and sold this game out of his garage, and did it as a part-time hobby, until he won some awards. Then it catapulted his business into his full-time passion and money maker. It was really inspiring to talk to him, as I feel many entrepreneurs can relate to his situation. Here is what Matt had to say about how awards have affected his hobby-turned-business.

Awards Turned My Part-Time Hobby Into My Full-Time Money Maker
Matt Butler: Owner, ROLLORS
Beavercreek, OH
www.rollors.net

Matt Shoup: *Tell me a little about your company and its growth over the past years.*

Matt Butler: *I originally started manufacturing and selling the ROLLORS game as a side business, and then we received some PR on our game. We used some strategies to land the free PR, and then things exploded. Right now, it is my full-time business, and it is hard to keep up with demand. We are a trademarked brand and have patents pending on the game.*

MS: *How are you keeping up from a distributing standpoint?*

MB: *We teamed up with a manufacturer in Wisconsin and also a have a licensing agreement for a distributor to sell our product. This way, we are less involved with the logistical aspect of the business. So far, we have sold around 40,000 games.*

MS: *So tell me how winning awards has come in to play for your company.*

MB: *One of the first awards we won was from **Dr. Toy** in 2010. **Dr. Toy** is one of the most prestigious organizations in the toy business, and each year they award toy companies awards for their games and toys. They have been around a long time, and have a deep-rooted credibility in our industry. They actually interact with parents and kids using and playing the games, and then are able to judge them. They awarded us one of the **Top 100 Games in 2010**, and we were awarded for being one of the **Top 10 Active Lawn Games in 2010**, as well. These were our first and most prestigious awards.*

MS: *So, these guys are the cream of the crop in your industry? Tell me more about what this award has done for you and the company.*

MB: *As I mentioned, these guys have clout in the industry. This is not just slapping a blue ribbon on your game. This award has launched our credibility in the industry, and other companies can see that we truly have an award-winning game on the market. It is also a benefit when potential buyers go to our website or see our game on the shelves. The biggest thing is the credibility and name recognition we receive. I never imagined that we would be so busy when I started this on the side, and awards have played a huge part in that growth.*

MS: *What have been some of the other benefits you have seen from winning awards?*

MB: *One of the other awards we won was from **Parenting Magazine** in Washington D.C., and there were 100,000 magazines circulating around. We were exposed to many parents, and people bought our game from winning this award and being mentioned in the magazine! That kind of exposure would be super expensive if done the traditional way, and here it was free.*

Another big benefit is that many of the special retail stores that carry our game also carry a lot of other award-winning games. They are more of the mom-and-pop-type stores, and many of the patrons of these stores are looking for award-winning games like mine. We have seen a large increase in sales in these stores from our awards. With this increase in sales, my business has scaled up, and I have taken it from a part-time hobby to a full-time passion that pays me!

MS: *What advice would you give to entrepreneurs seeking to win awards?*

MB: *Research and make sure you find the award that is a fit for you and your company. Remember that some awards may do more harm than good if they do not have the credibility to make your name stand out. The most credible ones will give you the most bang for your buck. You may not always win these at first try, but keep trying, and look into exactly what you need to do to win them. Keep at it.*

Also, remember that it is a big thing when you win an award! If you apply for one and win it, you deserve it. Be sure to celebrate it! Keep in mind the doors that will open and the opportunities you will have to be successful in business because of your awards. For me, this started as a hobby and part-time thing, and now we are big time.

WORKING IT OUT

- What were some of the major and reoccurring themes, benefits, and topics discussed by the entrepreneurs in these interviews?
- Did the size of business, revenue levels, or number of employees play a role into the effectiveness of the benefits, themes, etc.?
- Which entrepreneur do you and your business most closely relate to? Why?
- After reading these interviews, what advice continues to resonate with you?
- How will you apply this advice to your business to become an award-winning company?
- Do you agree with all the points mentioned in the interviews?

PART III:

More Benefits

CHAPTER 15

The Benefit of Standing Out From the Competition

If your business is anything like mine, the industry is filled with competitors battling to win business. Most companies are selling a similar product or service, so you will require something else that causes your company to shine. Being an award-winning company separates you from the competition.

Do you remember the guy or gal in high school that played sports and always lettered in their respective sport? They strutted down the hall proudly wearing their letter jacket to show that they were one of the best at what they did. They stood out in the crowd, and people knew who they were. Winning awards is no different.

When your company "letters," your website, your marketing, your team, and your brand are instantly equipped with a similar status and badge of legitimacy as you roll out into the market hunting for business. When you present yourself to vendors, potential and existing customers, and potential and existing team members, you bring with you tangible proof of your standing in the community, the state, the country, and even the world!

Remember though, you can't act like the knucklehead jock who lettered and then immediately started shoving kids into lockers. Being an award-winning company does not mean you can throw the basics of business out the window. You don't want to be the fat, bald, broke jock at your ten-year reunion! You want your business to have longevity and sustainability. So remember, if you are already showing the qualities of an award-winning company and letting your company speak for itself, as Curt Richardson says awards just confirm that your company is amazing.

I recently submitted an estimate against a competitor of mine, and the customer asked me: "What makes you different?" I answered honestly: "My competitor seems to provide a great quality job, has a warranty, and uses great products, but here is the one thing I know they don't offer." At that moment, I pulled out a packet that listed every one of the close to two dozen awards we have our name tied to. The customer's jaw almost hit the floor. He now realized that he was dealing with a company that was performing at a different level.

The customer was receiving bids from other local painting companies, and was having a hard time telling one from the next. I explained to him that *Inc. Magazine* and *Winning Workplaces* named us a *Top Small Workplace in 2011*, which meant that we have a happier, more dedicated and motivated team ready to serve him. Being a winning workplace means that we have lower turnover. I explained how that translates into better consistency in our product, and people who show up to his home excited to work. I was also able to mention that I was named one of *Colorado's Top 5 Young Professionals* by *ColoradoBiz Magazine* in 2010, because of the way I do business, the way I treat my team, and the way we give back to the community. After that, he was sold and excited for us to paint his home.

One thing to remember when you become an award winner is that you have to relate the award to why it benefits the customer. Don't just flash your trophy or sell sheet to them. Make them understand what it means to them (in benefits they receive) if they work with your award-winning company and WHY that's important. When you win an award, it is because the award organization voted that you were the best, biggest, top, winning, fastest, etc. in some category. This brings benefit to the customer, just make sure to connect those two points together or you're just being flashy.

WORKING IT OUT

Take out a sheet of paper or open a new Excel spreadsheet. In the first column, list the awards you have determined you are going to win. In the second column, list traits that describe your company in relation to this award. In the third list the benefits that these adjectives bring to your customers.

For example, if you were named a Top Workplace in your community (column 1), some descriptors of your company could be: consistent, positive company culture, high retention, low turnover, satisfied team, or great at taking care of people (column 2), and the benefits to the customer would be high quality products or services, security in knowing you will be around, positive people to do business with, working with those with integrity, or money well spent.

Just remember that you can list all of your selling points and cool marketing jargon for your potential customer, but you must also make the connection to show them how they will benefit from what you have. Once you determine the specific benefits of each award, you can consider how they specifically relate to your customer.

Win an Award

Describe the Qualities that Earned You This Award

The Sales Cycle of an Award-Winning Company ®

Close More Jobs

Describe How those Qualities Benefit the Customer

CHAPTER 16

The Benefit of Networking with Other Leaders

Get yourself some formal wear, because you are going to need it! When you become an award-winning company, you are suddenly among the elite. Winning awards brings with it free tickets to events, galas, dinners, and meet-and-greets associated with that award. Suddenly, you will be invited to meet and network with some of the most elite entrepreneurs in your city, state, country, and world. It is said that you become like the people with whom you spend time, so it is a great benefit to mingle with others who are striving for something excellent.

Besides the personal benefit and the intrinsic value of knowing noteworthy people, these events are awesome places to network. Your professional contact list will explode with people who have their own enormous contact lists that are suddenly at your disposal. I cannot even begin to explain the benefit to me personally and professionally of meeting people at these events. I would argue that the return is higher than any other possible investment in terms of the quality of people you meet for your hours spent. One of the big benefits Braun Mincher mentioned in his interview was being exposed to such a great group of elite people at a young age. These people not only knew him, but saw him as a credible leader.

At this point, it is crucial to understand that when you attend these events as an award-winner, you are most likely going to be held in high regard by the people you are meeting. This networking is different than the typical Chamber meet-and-greet, where you may not know the person you are about to talk to. There is a lot more ice to break and trust to build in that situation.

Remember one of the best tenets for business, networking, and life in general is to be available to serve others. The more you are able to help and serve others, the more things will come back to you in the long run.

Especially with people who have been around the block of business, you must know how to network well to take advantage of being introduced to these influential people. They can smell an amateur; so keep these pointers in mind:

- As Zig Ziglar has said, "If you help enough people get what they want, you will get what you want."
- When you initially meet someone, be genuine in your efforts to know them. The point initially is to gain a friend, mentor, and ally, not to seal a deal or sell something. Strive to make a simple follow-up appointment. It is at this meeting that you will both determine if working together will be mutually beneficial.
- Don't be a puker, that is a person who just spews information about him or herself, but brings no value to a business deal or interaction. You have two ears and only one mouth; use them in that proportion.
- Network for the person you are trying to get to know. Consider who you might be able to introduce to him or

her that might be able to help them in some way. Set up a time to make the introduction.

- Ask lots of questions. Engage each person by showing a genuine interest in them and their business, their goals, and their aspirations. People love to talk about themselves, and this information also benefits you as you learn from their lives.

WORKING IT OUT

Knowing that you will need to develop awesome networking skills, take some time to think about the following:

- At the last meet-and-greet you attended, did you seem to be more on the side of giving or receiving?
- Did you feel that you genuinely got to know the other people you met?
- Did you introduce any of these people to someone who could help them?
- Think of the last five people you met through networking. Now, think of one person you could introduce each of them who would benefit their agenda, and make those connections right now. Here is a sample script I like to use. This text is typed in an email that I send to both parties I am introducing:

Ted and Craig,

I just wanted to introduce you to each other, as I know you would both benefit from knowing each other.

Ted Jones is a business affiliate of mine and is currently working on helping companies with their hosted computer solutions. From his reputation and the companies I know he has helped, I can assure you that he runs a Rockstar company.

Craig Williams is the owner of ABC Solutions and a vendor for our company. ABC is the state's largest collection agency, and we have had a long and great relationship with them.

Craig, as we had coffee last week, I remembered you saying that you were exploring computer solutions. Ted is the best I know of for what you need. Ted, I imagine you might need Craig's expertise as you handle your own business affairs. I believe you could have a mutually beneficial relationship, so I will let you both take it from here.

Have a great day!

I also make sure to attach an electronic business card from each so they can easily save the other's information into their contacts.

Here are a few points to remember when making an introduction:

- Mention how you know each person being introduced.
- Show the benefit to each party of them meeting each other. Don't try to sell one thing for either side, just recommend they meet.
- Mention what each person does and how it will benefit the other.
- Throw in a kind word or two about each party.
- Attach electronic business cards.
- Let them take it from there!

Go ahead and do this right now. Yes! I mean right now. This is how these things get going—by seizing the present moment. So, put this book down, open up your email and fire them off! You'll thank me. The connections you make for others will tie you further into the larger community of business makers.

CHAPTER 17

The Benefit of Being an Industry Leader and Expert in Your Field

From speaking to and interviewing many top entrepreneurs and CEOs, as well as from my own personal experiences, I have learned that being an award-winning company puts you and your company out there as an industry leader and expert in your field. Because of this credibility, separation from the competition, an exposure to the public eye, many will approach you to ask your advice or opinion, or even to speak at an event.

Being an expert in your field, or even being perceived as one, can boost your exposure when it comes to speaking events. I have had the pleasure of being asked to speak at Chamber events, high school and university business events, conferences, and trainings about growing a successful company. All of this exposure as an expert brings back more business, credibility, and value to my company.

People want to hear advice from successful people, and being a BAAWC Rockstar will allow you to be that person. Each time you speak or get in front of other business owners or industry peers, it will boost your credibility and more connections and business will come out of it.

Working It Out

- How can you leverage the award you are going to win to become an expert in your field?
- Think specifically about what events, organizations, and groups could use your expertise and how you could bring benefits to them by the service you provide.
- If you don't have connections with these groups and organizations now, look at your contact and media list to see who you know that could help you get in touch with these groups.

PART IV:

*The 7 Simple Steps
and Other Tips for Becoming
an Award Winning Company*

CHAPTER 18

Award Winning Myths Set Straight

Are you inspired by the stories of the award-winning companies, and the benefits of being an award-winning company? Inspired enough to start winning some awards? I promise I'll get to the 7 Simple Steps soon, but first I want to dispel some of the myths associated with winning awards.

When I was only two years into my business, I picked up a newspaper and recognized a new local business that had just been named *Loveland's Top Small Company of the Year*. I remember automatically assuming that the same companies always win these things and that my company would never be recognized. It seemed obvious to me that you have to have the right people in your pocket to win those kinds of things. I put the paper down, and three years went by before I thought about it again.

In our interview, Greg Jenkins mentioned that many entrepreneurs feel their story or company is not good enough for an award. I had some of those false beliefs about how the awards industry works and those beliefs severely limited my business in becoming an award-winning company.

I'm sure you've heard the saying, "Whether you say you can or you say you can't, you are exactly right." No matter the scenario—a sales meeting, an investor pitch, an upset customer phone call—the story you create in your mind of what will happen many times comes true. Every time I go into a sale, I begin to think, "I am going to close this deal because these people will love me, trust me, and want to go with me." I am creating a vision of the outcome in my mind before it happens. I am setting the stage for the desired outcome.

Just as you can use the power of positive thinking for positive outcomes, your mind can also set the course for negative outcomes. A large part of being an award-winning company is the belief that you are that sort of company.

What outcomes are you creating in your mind right now?

WORKING IT OUT

- What stories are you creating in your head and what outcomes are those producing?
- Do they have a positive or negative outcome?
- Are you an award-winning company?
- If you are tempted to say, "no," is it true, or just in your head?
- If it is true, what action steps do you need to take in your business to change these things?

Don't waste any more time feeling left out of the award-winning crowd. It's time to debunk some myths and get your business on the awards roster!

Myth #1: The same companies win all the awards.

Why does it seem that a few companies win everything every year? Because it is generally true. But the reason has nothing to do with those companies being exclusively sought after. Those companies are winning awards because they follow the 7 Simple Steps outlined in this book. Award-winning companies win because they have intention. It is not just because of chance that the same companies win all the time. Once a company does win an award or two, a momentum starts to build, helping them to win more and more awards. The companies you see winning most often, at some point in time, merely unlocked the secret in this book. There is plenty of room for more companies in this arena, all they have to do is follow the steps spelled out in Chapter 19.

Myth #2: Awards come and find you.

About a year ago, I was sitting in my office working on a few proposals for a prospective client. My phone rang. It was Sally from *Inc. Magazine.* She explained how their organization had looked high and low for one of the top small workplaces in the country and, after much searching, they had found us! She was on the edge of her seat wanting to know: would I be willing to accept this prestigious award?

Just kidding! I wish that were true. How great would it be if you could just go about your daily business and be hunted down to accept awards? Awards work like all the scholarships you had to apply for in high school. They were not just handed out; you had to go find them, not the other way around. There are a few instances in which some industries will search down and present an award to you, but 99% of the time, this is not the case.

Myth #3: People who win awards know the right people.

I used to think that the companies that won these awards all the time just knew somebody that worked for the magazine or organization offering the award. I was wrong about that too. As I continued to win awards, I found there is no truth to that at all.

None of the 7 Simple Steps involve knowing the right people. You do not need an uncle who is the CEO of the publication giving the award. You do not have to know the judges to give you a good plug or a foot in the door.

Myth #4: You have to pay to win awards.

You do not need to bribe anyone or advertise with any particular publication in order to win an award. For some awards, there are minimal application fees associated with the basic costs of processing your application, but outside of clear-cut fees, winning awards does not require slipping someone a "Benjamin."

Myth #5: Why would they want to honor me?

I, along with many other entrepreneurs, have asked "why would they give ME this award?" Let me tell you another secret.

In 2010, M & E Painting was nominated for a very prestigious national business award. The ritzy awards gala was in New York City. We stayed in Times Square and rubbed elbows with some of the nation's top entrepreneurs and business owners. We drank expensive wine and dined on some killer filets. There was even gold-leafed chocolate cake for dessert.

A single ticket to our own awards ceremony cost $450! And, that price didn't cover airfare, our hotel, or the associated expenses. There were over 2,000 people at that event, so the dinner alone generated close to $1 million in revenue for the awards organization. There were other ways you could spend money too. You could advertise in the bulletin, or be named and advertised as a sponsor for the event if you chose.

I just said you don't need to pay to win awards, and this is true. Understand that the award industry is a **for-profit business**. Asking the question, "Why would anyone want to give me an award?" is kind of like asking, "Why would I want my customers to do business with me?" Because there is a profit to be made, that's why!

Here is the secret within the secret: Awards want you more than you want them!

Awards and award events are big business. Award-giving is an industry that generates gigantic revenues and profits for hosting organizations and publications. Now you may be thinking that just devalues the award, but let's face it, the awards industry is a win-win-win business. The host earns profits and builds connections to highly influential entrepreneurs. You are already familiar with the list of benefits that the award-winner receives. Numerous vendors and businesses – from the hotels to the caterers, printers and beyond – benefit from the extra business as well.

So now we have taken care of the myths. I hope you are inspired to read the next chapter to find out exactly how to go out and win some awards.

WORKING IT OUT

- Write down any preconceptions you may have about winning awards.
- What do you feel is holding you back from becoming an award-winning company?
- What kind of companies do you feel win awards consistently?
- Right now, do you feel like you can become an award-winning company?
- Why or why not?

CHAPTER 19

The 7 Simple Steps
to Become an Award Winning Company

So here they are, the ever so important, yet simple, seven steps. It's is important for you realize that these steps must be followed to a T. Like any system, it is only as effective as the person implementing it. I am going to keep this section short, sweet, and to the point, and make sure you know exactly what to do and how to do it.

Steps 1 through 6 show you how to arrive to the awards podium, and Step 7 shows you how to leverage this success once you do. The cool thing about these steps is that they don't take a lot of time (maybe 15 minutes per day), and they are completely duplicatable and easy to teach to others.

Step 1: Decide to become a BAAWC Rockstar.

Before you can do any of the next steps, you need to make the decision that you are going to become an award-winning company. You need to believe that you are an award winner before you have won any awards. As I've already mentioned, a BAAWC Rockstar does not need evidence before belief. So right here, right now, decide that you are going to win awards.

Sounds simple enough, and some may ask why this is even a step. Based on my experience, as well as talking to other award-winning companies, this is indeed a very important step and the first step in winning. Without getting yourself into the right mind-set, you can go through the motions of the next steps and nothing will happen.

Step 2: You can't win if you don't play. Search, List, Qualify, and Apply.

Now that you have decided to become an award winner, the second step is to search, list, qualify, and apply. There is no possibility of winning an award for which you haven't applied or been nominated. It is up to you to go out and find awards. The more you apply for, the more you win. When I first started, I applied for four awards and was named a finalist for two. I didn't win anything, but I saw how the process worked.

A few months later, I applied for two more awards, was named a finalist for one, and won the other. As nice as it would be to win them all, you don't. Like so many things, winning awards is a numbers game. Remember Greg Jenkins' interview? He said that practice makes perfect, and the same is true for multiple entries. Your awards packet will improve each time you enter.

Search

Understanding you need to apply for the award is great, but where do you go to find these awards? Of course, the Internet is an endless supply of leads. Any search engine is a gateway to numerous awards. Type in "business awards" along with your state, city, region, or industry. Now make a list of the awards that you are going to apply for from these searches.

Keep your eyes open for notices of other companies winning awards in the media, then search for those awards by name to learn how to apply. While you are in search mode, you will be amazed at how many awards have been right under your nose.

In Appendix I is a list of awards for which I have been nominated and have won. You can use this list as a starting point for your research. Another great source is trade organizations specific to your industry.

List

Create an Excel spreadsheet of possible awards, that you can update as you apply, re-apply, and win. Some columns you might want to include are: Award Name, Application Open, Application Due Date, Qualifications, Do I Qualify?, Entry Cost, Information Needed, Research of Past Winners, Entered?, Confirmed?, Finalist?, and Won?. Arrange this list in order of application deadline dates. Keeping this list organized and frequently updated is crucial to winning as many awards as possible.

Qualify

Make sure you check the criteria of the awards to see if it is realistic for you to apply for them. If you don't qualify, go to the next one, but keep it on your list for when you attain the qualification criteria. Some qualifiers may include number of employees, years in business, and revenue levels.

Apply

Read the application instructions carefully, and follow them to the letter. Don't make the mistake of thinking you are an exception, someone to whom the rules don't apply. If they ask for one type of document, don't send another type, no matter how closely they are related. Be sure to leave yourself enough time to go through the process. Don't rush it. Instead, spend the time to carefully fill out the application, and tell a story the judges will want to read. Have a few team members review your application before it's turned in and ask them to assume the role of the judges. Let them poke holes in your application before you turn it in.

Step 3: Have a story that appeals to the award, and tell it well.

Apply for many awards and apply often, but don't just throw mud at the wall to see what sticks. Remember how Kristen Tatti with OtterBox mentioned the sniper rifle approach to applying for awards? You can still apply often, but make sure you have focus and can laser in on each award to win it.

As you search through awards, consider what element of your own business story appeals to each specific award. I don't recommend stretching to apply for an award that there is no chance you will get. If you are applying for a fastest growing company award and you don't have the numbers to prove that you are growing rapidly, then you are wasting valuable time that you could be spending on a relevant award (or rapidly growing your company).

Mine the questions on the application for clues as to the relevancy of the award for your business. If you can answer them with a story from your journey, then you are on the right track. And do tell your story. Every award has someone (or several people) chosen to read application after application.

Don't just answer the question; give them something that will help them remember you. If you've thought of some great adjectives to describe your business, chances are, so has every other business owner. What others don't have is your unique story.

All awards will ask for some kind or narrative about why you are deserving of the award. It could have to do with your innovation, growth, contribution to the community, workplace, culture, etc. Be sure you sell your story and make it stand out in the crowd. Also make certain you give the award organizations exactly what they ask for. Do not deviate from what they ask you to turn in. Lot of companies have a great story to share but the ones who win know what that story is and clearly and convincingly tell it.

WORKING IT OUT

As preparation, answer these potential award questions:
- Tell us why your company is unique and innovative in your industry?
- What obstacles and challenges has your company faced and overcome?
- Tell us some unique things that make your workplace stand out?

- How does your company compare to your competitors?
- How has the current economic climate affected your business, and how have you handled those changes?
- What is your business doing to contribute to the community?
- What are your long term-plans and vision for your company?
- Above all this, what is your story? Is it an amazing one? Have you told it yet? How often? What are the selling points of your story? What makes it unique?
- Write your story:
    o Write about getting into your business. What did you do before?
    o What were some of the challenges of starting your business?
    o What were some lessons learned?
    o Talk about the turning points in the business, or big realizations.
    o What makes your company unique in the market?

People love to hear a success story that goes against all odds. Award judges are no exception.

Answering many of the questions an awards organization might ask will help you to develop and craft your story.

When I started my company, I had no idea that the initial $100 deposit I made in my bank account would be so crucial to developing and creating my story. You may be doing things in your business right now that are going to be key points in your story, so keep this in mind.

Search for past winners of the awards you aspire to win. Find their biographies and look for trends and similarities between award winners. In this way, you get inside the "mind" of that particular award organization to discover what most appeals to them. Obviously, you must avoid plagiarism. The idea is not to take their ideas, but to determine what made them appealing, find similarities in your own story, and build your answers around those common traits.

Brainstorm a list of topics, stories, and pitches. Begin to think about how they could work for numerous different angles. The fundraiser you held last year might cover your community involvement and be a great answer for any question about your philanthropy, but it also might work for a question about team dynamics to show the service-oriented nature of your staff, or their ability to coordinate well outside the work walls.

Remember, have a great story, tell it well, and be sure to give the judges exactly what they ask for.

Step 4: Hire a great editor.

When I first began to apply for awards, I was not winning any of them. My wife read an essay I had just used for an application and yelled, "It's no wonder you didn't win – this is awful!" She gave it back to me with lots of red marks and comments. I had sent that one out with nobody looking it over other than me. I just wonder what the judges thought. Not much, I'm sure, because I didn't make it past the first round.

Your editor can make the difference between losing and winning an award. I remember receiving back a proofed copy of an essay response for a specific award I was eager to apply for. It was transformed, and I knew right away that it was a winner. An amazing editor will not only correct grammar and structural issues. They will also make sure your story flows and that your voice is heard and consistent throughout.

Remember, you want a story that jumps off the page and stands apart from the crowd. The judges should not be able to put it down. They should want to keep it at the top of the pile. Having a great story is your job, but your editor's job is to tell that story in a way that great storytellers do—in a way that creatively and persuasively captivates your audience.

How do you find a great editor? Ask around at lead and networking groups, or post an interest on social networking sites. Try a few at first. When you apply for your first awards, have two or three editors work on the same piece and look for one whose style appeals to you. You should also be sure that their "voice" matches yours to avoid sounding phony, touched up, or not like you at all.

Using an editor costs a little bit of money, but is well worth it. Once I started having my award applications edited well, I started winning awards.

WORKING IT OUT

Brainstorm a list of editors you know, or people or resources to lead you to an editor. If you have not begun to apply for awards, send an email correspondence, a newsletter or the text for your latest advertising flyer to an editor. Does their voice match your style? Does the work still seem like it is yours? Are there noticeable improvements? Make sure the person you choose is easy to work with and understands your goals. Is this someone who can represent you well?

Step 5: Follow up and follow through.

Business can't happen until a sale is made. Clearly, sales are crucial for any company's success. A large part of success in the sales process is follow-up. When submitting award applications, you are selling yourself and your business. After you submit an application, many awards will send you an auto response email as a receipt. Many will include the information of a contact person. Send a hand-written thank you card to that person, and let them know of your appreciation for the opportunity to apply for the award. If possible, follow up with a phone call to make sure they received any attachments, and ask if they have any questions about your entry.

During one such call, I discovered that, though I electronically submitted my application and got the auto response saying it had been received, the application in fact had not come through. We went on to win this award proving it was worth the time I took to follow up.

WORKING IT OUT

I already talked about the Excel spreadsheet you can make to track your progress in Step 2. Be sure to include a few more columns to track who the main contact is for the award, and what date you followed up on, as well as any notes about the conversation. Also be sure you have a column for the date the award will be announced so you can check back to see if you are a winner.

Step 6: Don't give up.

Even after you've become an award-winning professional, you are not going to win every award. There is tough competition out there, and you may not be noticed the first time you apply. The best thing to do is keep trying. I have found that being named a finalist for an award one year makes me more likely to win the next year. This was the case for us with our *Inc. Magazine* and *Winning Workplaces Top Small Workplace* applications. Perseverance makes you visible. Remaining in front of people pays off. Keep in mind that applying for an award and not winning it will give you excellent exposure to the process of that particular application, and you will know what to expect the next year.

Another point to consider is that the mind-set you have as you prepare, organize, and turn in your award applications is very important. Do you see yourself walking across that stage as an award winner? Do you really know and truly believe you are an award-winning company? As you tell yourself you are an award winner throughout the process, that positive and winning energy is transferred into your award presentations. The voice that comes across is the voice of a winner.

Kody Bateman, CEO of SendOutCards, and author of the book *Promptings*, always makes the point that the story in your mind becomes the story of your life. What is the story of your company that you are telling yourself and creating? Is it that of an award winner? Remember, even when people who always think positively and believe they are winners lose, they are still winners. They continue to try, and don't give up. Remember this as you apply for awards. Keep at it, keep telling yourself you're a winner, and you will be one.

Step 7: When you win, share it with the world.

If you follow these first six steps, you will win awards. In the process, you probably invested several hours of time in answering questions and in follow-up, and perhaps a small amount of money for editing. Now get ready to take advantage of the thousands of dollars of exposure it will bring you! There will most likely be an awards gala that you can attend with members of your company. Take the time to celebrate with those who helped make your company worthy of this award.

It is also crucial that you now take the time to leverage this award to its full potential to bring free press, media exposure, recognition, and benefits to your business. This is where the seventh step comes in. Don't forget to work this step. The first six are the steps that make you an award winner, and the seventh is what you do after to maximize the benefits. Here are some of the ways you can share this award with the world:

1. Send a press release to the local media (newspapers, radio stations, television), and follow up with a phone call to show your determination to share your story. Phone calls are great because reporters and press receive press releases all day long.

2. Another thing you can do with the press to get more recognition is to pitch a story relating to a hot topic in the news. For example, maybe your business can demonstrate "how a company creates amazing culture in a down economy." If a story like this is written about you, it is likely the writer will also mention your award. Remember, when one paper, or publication gets a hold of your story, others will follow.

3. Once you get one story in a particular publication, call others and mention you have an awesome story to share. Specifically say, "The Daily Times (or whoever else just wrote about you) just wrote a story about this." All media outlets want to keep up with each other, so bring published stories to their attention, and your story might just run in numerous media outlets.

4. Don't limit yourself to the newspaper, but think of all media outlets, including TV, blogs, radio, etc. If one writes about you, talks about you, or records you, the others will want to as well.

5. Make an Excel list of media contacts and pitches, dates pitched, stories done, follow-up, etc. Use this list the same way you used the awards list to track awards.

6. Post announcements on all social media sites. Ask your friends and online connections to share or repost your announcements. This will help with your SEO rankings.

7. Speaking of SEO rankings, many of the awards organizations will post your story and tag your name, company, website, etc. on their page. This will help with SEO as well. Another thing I have done is create an awards section on my website and link to the awards sites from there. You can do this as well, to give the awards organizations some exposure, and also show your customers and people who visit your website that you are a winner.

8. Send a mass email to your distribution and client list (leveraging your connections and contacts) to express your excitement. Share links to get people navigating to your website and the awards website.

9. Throw a celebration party at your place of business and invite customers, vendors, and team members. You can invite the media to this event as well. We hosted a barbeque on October 29, 2010, for winning a *Colorado Companies to Watch* Award. I remember the date well, as I missed the event because my beautiful daughter was born that day. We invited the mayor of our city, media, customers, vendors, and family. I heard that it was an amazing event, and know it drew lots of buzz and attention, and got people talking about us.

10. Mail out a thank you note to particular clients for helping your company succeed in winning each award. I recommend not selling or offering anything else with the information other than the fact that you were a winner.

11. Make sure you also send a message to **halloffame@baawc.com** so I can highlight you on my website. This section of the site will highlight all of my BAAWC Rockstars and the awards they have won. This is just another way to help you share your success with the world.

WORKING IT OUT

When you win your first award, how will you share it with the world? What are some of the methods and media you will use? Do you have your contact list developed in order to do so? What methods of mass contact and database management will you use?

Use the natural momentum of the buzz. When you get excited, your enthusiasm will become contagious. After one of our prestigious wins, our outdoor advertising company surprised us with a very generous gift. They posted two billboards in very prominent areas in Fort Collins and Loveland announcing our award and congratulating us on our success. I know these billboards sell for close to $1,000 per month, but they designed and posted those billboards for free as a client appreciation present. Don't be shy when it comes to sharing your accomplishment. If you've won an award, you merit that acclaim and the free attention that comes with it. Remember that your team and your clients share in this success, so don't hold back from letting everyone enjoy the benefits of your victory!

Let's recap the 7 Simple Steps to Become An Award Winning Company:

1. **Decide to become a BAAWC Rockstar.**
2. **You can't win if you don't play. Search, List, Qualify, and Apply.**
3. **Have a story that appeals to the award, and tell it well.**
4. **Hire a great editor.**
5. **Follow up and follow through.**
6. **Don't give up.**
7. **When you win, share it with the world.**

So that's it. Those are the seven steps to becoming an award winner. Keep the process as simple as I showed you, and you will succeed. Before we get into the tips I share with you in the next chapter, I want to give you a word of caution that you must know now that you are about to enter award winning territory.

A Note of Caution

Be prepared for a whole new level of exposure that will come to you and your company from winning awards. Because of this exposure, you will also be the proud recipient of more solicitations! Curt Richardson with OtterBox definitely confirmed this in his interview. Your contact information will be everywhere. That is a really, really good thing for business, but it means that you will be the target for people who will want your business as well.

Be very careful to whom you choose to respond. I rarely do business with people who cold call me by pulling my name from an awards list. Develop a method to quickly end such calls and don't feel bad about sending those letters straight to the dumpster. Your time is valuable and you want to continue to work with people who recognize that and take the time to make legitimate business connections. Learn to tell the difference between cold callers and people wanting to know you, connect with you, and create mutually beneficial relationships. These people will quickly set themselves apart from those who just want to sell you something.

Once you have made those connections, you will quickly realize that it is your duty to live up to the increased expectations that come with being a BAAWC Rockstar. If you are not ready to exceed those higher expectations, then I would hold off on this process.

CHAPTER 20

Tips for the BAAWC Rockstar

Here are some rules and ways I run my business that, I guarantee if you follow, you can't go wrong. Some of them were already mentioned as I described what it takes to be a BAAWC Rockstar and what it truly means to be one. Try taking one item per week and really focusing on it. Write it down, and focus on it entirely. Once you get good at one, try another. Be careful to not try and do it all at once. You may already be doing some of these things; if so, great!

I am only going to share a few tips here, because I don't want to get away from the main point that, as an award-winning company, you are going to be able to go out and attain massive success, exposure, credibility, free PR, and more business, and enjoy all the benefits I have written about throughout this book. I do feel it is important for BAAWC Rockstars to always try to improve their businesses. So, here are my top five tips. Watch for the rest in my next book!

Have a clear why. Know it, write it down, share it, live it.

Some of the most amazing feats in history have been accomplished by a leader with a clear why and a clear vision for where they are going. In Chapter 3, I talked about why I wrote this book. Sure, it is about winning awards—that's the what—but the why is that I want to inspire entrepreneurs. When things get tough, people will stick with you if you have a strong why; if you don't, they won't.

Once you are clear on your why, you can share it with others. As you begin to share your why, you may have some people leave your organization; GREAT! This will inspire the people that stay with you even more because they believe in you and your vision.

Never underestimate the power of vision and a strong why behind it. When a business and its leader have one and it is clear, the sky is the limit.

Never budge on your values.

Let me share from experience that a BAAWC Rockstar has values for a reason. What are the core values you run your business by? Are they clear? Are they stated and listed out just like your why and your vision? If not, take some time and list them out now. What do you value about the way you do business? If you value timeliness, hold yourself and your team accountable to demonstrate this value always. If you value friendliness, make sure to reward those who show up to work with a smile.

Don't ever budge on the values that are important to you in the interest of making a few extra bucks. "Well I guess it's okay that he was late; I mean he is our top sales guy." I hear that one all the time. How about, "We can let it slide just this one time, while we are working on this big account."

Your company runs on a certain set of core values, and if you are seen as a wishy-washy leader who adheres to those values only when it's convenient or profitable, your team will see it, and that inconsistency will set you up for disaster. Let your yes be your yes, and your no be your no—always, plain and simple. Also understand that sticking to your values will sometimes cost you money, but will ultimately make you more in the long run by upholding your integrity and good business name.

Get a rant or a rave, just get them talking about you.

A business that nobody talks about will eventually die off. One of the worst things that can happen in your business is when you work for a customer and they give you no feedback. Having open dialogue and creating situations for feedback is key. One of the sections of my www.baawc.com website is the Rant and Rave section (under the Blog dropdown). Since I understand the value of feedback in my business, I give feedback to other businesses.

In the Rant and Rave section, I video blog about companies I am a raving fan of. For example, after an office fire in September 2011, we were blessed to be surrounded by and connected to amazing companies that served us beyond our wildest expectations, so I blogged about them. In the video I thanked them for their service and posted the videos on their social media pages. They were absolutely thrilled to get these testimonials. Point being, those business owners know where their company stands with me: I love them and I am a raving fan.

On the other hand, it is valuable to get some negative feedback and constructive criticism from a customer once in a while too. You can always do something more to serve customers, and knowing what those things are will make your company better. Handling it is the key. Don't take it personally. If there is something you could have done better, accept that feedback, appreciate it, and make it right. If I am unhappy with a product or service, and I bring it to the attention of a company, and they handle it well, I will be a raving fan.

If you ever experience a positive raving review, thank your customer for it, assure them that you will continue to do business that way, and let them know how much you appreciate their feedback. What about a rant? Handle it the same way. Thank the customer for their feedback, but assure them you will fix the issue they are upset about.For me, it is actually really cool to get negative feedback or approach a customer who is unhappy with us, and make it right for them.

Getting a rant is your opportunity to shine and show customers how much ownership, accountability, and responsibility you will take. Here is a tip, though: When you get a rant or an unhappy customer, make sure you deal with the issue at hand.

I recently had a window well cover company come out to install a window well cover on my new deck. We had worked with this company once before, and my wife and I were very impressed with the owner. There were a few hiccups during the first experience, but they took care of everything immediately.

The second time around was a different story. We were told that the installer would be there on a certain day, at a certain time, and he wasn't. We received no call from them to explain why, and that was our main concern: **You said you would be there and then weren't.**

I expressed this concern clearly to the owner, and he followed up by taking accountability for everything else other than the fact that they no-call-no-showed on us. He went on in pages and pages of worthless emails about how he had to test his tech with trial by fire, and how I was a business owner, so I should know what he means. He never just accepted accountability for his guy not showing up when he said he would. All he had to do was that, and I would be referring him all day long.

So I told him this in an email back to him (since he didn't give his cell phone number to customers), and he then responded with an email back to me telling me a thing or two about what a great business man he is, and how he gave me a free window well lock kit for my troubles, and what a low profit margin industry he is in, and how one of his friends used my painting company and was not happy. The content of his email was unnecessary and still did not take accountability for the issue at hand, which was: **they said they would be there and weren't.**

He took the path of blame, excuses, and denial, as well as trying to divert the business issue between us and make it an issue between my company and one of his friends.

Remember, things can get heated, emotional, and difficult when issues arise, but get to the main issue and WHY the customer is upset, then deal with it.

Too many businesses are scared to get negative feedback,

so they would rather get none. BIG MISTAKE. I have been there and done that before and learned the hard way. A large percentage of people that are not happy with you will just not do business with you again, and never say anything. It is up to you to ask your customers for feedback, and then when they give it to you, accept it, good or bad. Just don't leave them not talking about you or to you at all.

Don't catch the Bad Economy Disease: (BED) bug.

There is a very contagious, dangerous, and deadly disease being spread through the entrepreneurial community right now. It is called Bad Economy Disease, also known as the BED bug. That's right, it became airborne in 2008, and has infected tens of thousands (maybe more) of entrepreneurs across the country and world. Once caught, it quickly spreads through all members of an organization. If not treated, it can kill a business quickly.

There is a way to avoid this disease, or (if you are already feeling its symptoms) to cure it. The remedy is administered by self-vaccination, and the cool thing is, you don't need to prick yourself with a needle. All you have to do is say, right now, "I will not catch the BED bug!" Then, say it again every day, because others who are infected by it will spit their germs at you daily as you meet and do business with them. It is impossible to avoid all who have been affected by this disease, but it is recommended that you stay away from them as much as possible.

The truth is there is no bad economy out there. Well, not for you if you are a BAAWC Rockstar, that is. Here's a little tip: Go out and happen to the world, and don't sit back and let the "big bad economy" beat you up and push you around. I get very frustrated when I hear business owners talk about how business is bad because of the economy. "We are affected by fuel prices, cost of commodities, we are a luxury item, blah, blah, blah." I am not here to overlook the millions of people who have lost jobs or the many businesses that are suffering, but let me share this story to illustrate, as this is the story I hear repeatedly from entrepreneurs who have caught this deadly disease.

I sat down for coffee with a contractor who is in the concrete business. We caught up for a little bit on how life was going, how business was, and then he dropped the words I have heard all too frequently for the past three years: "Matt, we are getting killed in this economy, business really sucks right now, and it is a struggle." I let those words sink in for a minute and then we had the following conversation:

Me: *What books have you read lately? Have you learned anything new, attended a seminar, maybe listened to a book on CD?*
Him: *None, really.*
Me: *So what are you learning?*
Him: *Nothing, I guess. I do know the economy sucks.*
Me: *So what are you going to do about it?*
Him: *What do you mean? I can't do anything about it.*
Me: *So when things are good, why are they good?*
Him: *Well, because the economy is good.*
Me: *So, your success is only related to the economy, and nothing you do?*
Him: *[silence]*
Me: *Tell me about what you are doing to reach out to your*

customers? What is your business plan for growth in the bad economy? What is your cost per lead? Are you taking advantage of the bad economy to win some free PR? Are you tracking your sales? Are you tracking your profit? How exactly are you getting "killed by the economy"? What are the metrics you track to determine the health of your business? What does your sales process look like? How are you making yourself stand out from others to win and retain more business in this economy? Who else are you helping, serving, and making strategic partnerships with to win in this economy? If the economy wasn't an issue, what would your plan look like?

He sat there very quietly, yet leaned forward while he sipped his latte. I then asked him the question I would encourage every entrepreneur to ask themselves if they are rundown and suffering from the BED bug: "What do you think your competitor, ABC Concrete, has done to consistently grow and be successful in this similar bad economy?"

This is what this so-called bad economy does every time it happens. It separates entrepreneurs that are good from those that are great. Every bad economy has a story of success, growth, and innovation that happens within a company, no matter what is happening around it. The excuse of a bad economy cannot be used if there is even one company in your industry that shines during this time, think Southwest Airlines.

The BED bug is a killer because it creates an easy excuse to not make things happen in your business. It takes control away from you, and leaves your business success or business failure completely up to the economy. Companies that are great and that follow the BAAWC Rockstar code can answer all of the above questions, as well as those in the WORKING IT OUT sections throughout this book. They can also answer these questions as they relate to the "bad economy."

My main point is that if you wake up and decide business will automatically be bad, it will. If you decide the economy will affect you in a bad way, it will. You can also choose the glass-is-half-full approach, which says, we are going to take advantage, grow, make a name for ourselves, get some free PR, and win awards and more business BECAUSE of the bad economy.

People are still spending money, they just may have different motivations for how and when they spend it, and it is up to BAAWC Rockstars to figure this out. So please don't catch the BED bug!

Empower your team to make decisions without you based on values.

No matter where you are in your business right now, empowering your team is crucial. Many business owners are slaves to their business. This unfortunate situation can happen either intentionally (because the entrepreneur wants to control everything), or unintentionally, based on the culture and operation of the company revolving around the leader. One of the things in my business that has truly freed me is empowering my team to make decisions. If I have shared my vision correctly, the team will know what I will decide and, more importantly, why I will decide it.

I challenge you, after you close this book, to not answer a single team member's question for the next 30 days. "I have a question about collecting on the Jones account." "What should I do about this upset customer?" "This order came in wrong and has now backed up production." Whatever the questions is, I want you to respond to it with the exact words, "What do you think you should do?" or, "What do you think I would do, and why?"

As entrepreneurs and business owners, our teams look to us for leadership, approval, and inspiration. Often, this means they bring everything to our attention as well. If you are that crucial in the operations of your business, then you are a slave to your business. Unempowered team members cannot work to their full potential either. I am a natural micromanager and a control freak. This concept has always been a hard one for me to grasp and, honestly, I do not always do it 100% of the time. However, when I do, business always runs the smoothest and most effective.

So take the 30-day challenge of not answering any questions, see what kinds of decisions your team makes, and find out why they made them. When they explain, ask them "why" again. Have them explain why over and over until you find the true why, which will be the main core value that that decision was made for. Make sure it's in alignment with the company's core values. When you know your team understands the company's core values, you can step away and know things can run without you.

CHAPTER 21

Conclusion

At the beginning of this book, I promised it would be worth the money you spent and that this book would be a powerful one to have in your collection. So is it? Do you feel like this concept, and applying these 7 Simple Steps will add significant amounts of money to your bottom line? Did you make the commitment to become a BAAWC Rockstar? If so, the only next thing to do is to go apply the 7 Simple Steps and win some awards.

Set some time aside in the coming days and weeks to work through the workbook and apply the concepts and simple steps into your business. Make sure to consistently have a purpose, plan, and goals, and I guarantee you will succeed.

Make a commitment right now that 12 months from now you will have (fill in the number) awards next to your company's name, and then go out and get them. Be sure to keep me posted \when you win your first, second, third, fifth and tenth awards. Do this by sending me an email to **halloffame@baawc.com**. There is a section of the **www.BAAWC.com** website just for you that will highlight your success and get your business even more exposure. As more and more BAAWC Rockstars win awards, I will feature them on the website in many different ways, so be on the lookout for that.

I am proud of you for joining the BAAWC Rockstar Community. Remember, you are not alone. There are hundreds, thousands, and soon to be millions of BAAWC Rockstars that have also joined us. We are all here to support each other, inspire each other, and serve each other. Make sure, if you haven't already, to start contributing to the BAAWC blog. This blog is designed for two reasons. First, it is designed for you to share advice and receive advice from other BAAWC Rockstars. Second, by contributing, you will receive tons of FREE PR, as other BAAWC Rockstars and site visitors see what you, the expert, has to say.

I hope you have enjoyed your time reading this book as much as I have enjoyed writing it. I can't wait to hear from you and for you to share with me how you became an award-winning company!

APPENDIX I:
MATT'S COMPANIES

M & E Painting, LLC
540 W. 66th St. B1
Loveland, CO 80538
www.mandepainting.com
(970) 207-1005 office
(970) 613-0772 fax

M & E Painting was founded by Matt Shoup in March of 2005. Since then, the company has become the largest and leading residential and commercial repainting contractor in Northern Colorado. Their mission is simple: to serve their customers, team, and community with excellence. Having served over 5,000 customers and completed $14 million worth of painting in only nine years, Matt and M & E Painting are sought out by other businesses, as well as the local, state, and national media for its success. The majority of M & E Painting's growth was accomplished during the down economy, and of course, M & E Painting is an award winning company.

Here are the awards that M & E Painting and Matt Shoup have been named finalists and/or winners of:

Professional Awards for Matt Shoup

- 2013 – *Northern Colorado Business Report* – Named to 40 Under 40 Leaders Honor Roll
- 2012 – *Colorado State University* – Distinguished Alumni GOLD Award Winner- named as Graduate of the Last Decade.
- 2012 – *Stevie Awards* – Bronze American Business Award Winner as Executive of the Year
- 2010 – *ColoradoBiz Magazine* – Named one of the Top 5 Most Influential Young Professionals in Colorado
- 2010 – *Northern Colorado Business Report* – Named one of Northern Colorado's 30 Rising Stars
- 2009 – *Northern Colorado Business Report* – Nominated for 40 Under 40 Award
- 2009 – Loveland Chamber of Commerce – Finalist for Heart Award
- 2009 – Fort Collins Chamber of Commerce – Finalist for Young Professional of the Year Award

Awards for M & E Painting

- 2013 – *Stevie Awards* – Bronze American Business Award Winner for Company of the Year.
- 2011 – *Inc. Magazine* and Winning Workplaces – Top Small Company Workplace
- 2011 – *Inc. 5000* – #2705 of America's Fastest Growing Private Companies
- 2011 – *Stevie Awards* – Finalist for Business of the

Year (category: Up to 100 Employees)

- 2011 – *Northern Colorado Business Report* – #78 on the Mercury 100 List of Northern Colorado's Fastest Growing Companies
- 2011 – *Wall Street Journal* – Nominated for Small Business, Big Innovation Award
- 2011 – Best in Biz Awards – Bronze Winner for Most Customer Friendly Company of the Year
- 2010 – American Business Awards – Finalist for Business of the Year (category: Up to 100 Employees)
- 2010 – *Northern Colorado Business Report* – #8 on the Mercury 100 List of Northern Colorado's Fastest Growing Companies
- 2010 – *Inc. Magazine and* Winning Workplaces – One of 40 Finalists for the Top Small Company Workplaces Award
- 2010 – *ColoradoBiz Magazine* – Named 1 of 50 Colorado Companies to Watch
- 2010 – *Inc. 5000* List – #1724 of America's Fastest Growing Private Companies
- 2010 – ColoradoBiz Magazine – #243 of Colorado's Top 250 Private Companies
- 2010 and 2011 – Angie's List – Super Service Award
- 2009 – Loveland Chamber of Commerce – Finalist for Business of the Year Award
- 2009 – Loveland Chamber of Commerce – Finalist for Survivor Award

M & E Painting is continuing to grow and maintain its foothold as Northern Colorado's leading painting company, and also one of Northern Colorado's companies that gives back to and serves its community.

Free Paint Makeover Program

The M & E Painting Free Paint Makeover Program was initiated in 2009. M & E Painting searches for and wants to hear the stories of people whose homes need painting but who cannot afford to have them painted. The Free Paint Makeover team interviews these people and families, and decides which houses to paint for free. If you or anyone you know could use this program, please email: freepaintmakeover@mandepainting.com.

To date, M & E Painting has served seven families in Colorado with this campaign, and plans to serve more in the years to come.

The M & E Painting story has become synonymous with the ability for an entrepreneur to attain the American dream and serves as an inspiration to many across Colorado, the nation, and the entrepreneurial world.

Shoup Consulting, LLC

540 W. 66th St. B1
Loveland, CO 80538
www.mattshoup.com
(970) 372-1920 office
(970) 613-0772 fax

Matt Shoup founded Shoup Consulting in 2009, with the vision and mission to inspire entrepreneurs all over the world. Matt's passion for entrepreneurship and the value he places on entrepreneurs and their ability to change the world is what drives him to inspire as many entrepreneurs as he can. Matt does this in many forms, including individual and group coaching and mentoring, seminars, speaking engagements, and of course by authoring his first book (of many more to come), *Become an Award Winning Company*. Matt offers his services to entrepreneurs and organizations all over the globe.

Follow Matt and his companies:

www.mandepainting.com

www.facebook.com/mandepainting

www.mattshoup.com

www.facebook.com/shoupconsulting

www.becomeanawardwinningcompany.com or baawc.com

www.facebook.com/becomeanawardwinningcompany.com

www.facebook.com/matt.shoup

www.twitter.com/mattshoup

www.linkedin.com/in/mattshoup

APPENDIX II:
RESOURCES

The Infamous BAAWC Site

As mentioned, the Become an Award Winning Company website (www.baawc.com) is more than just an informational website about my book. This site is the meeting place for all BAAWC Rockstars, where we gather to learn how to become a better company, win awards, and inspire each other. So make sure, if you haven't already, that you go to the site, and click on the star that says "FREE WORKBOOK." I will send you weekly blog requests and opportunities to receive some free PR and exposure for your business. At the same time, you will be inspiring all the other BAAWC Rockstars. This site will also be a place for companies to learn more about the BAAWC Rockstar Community, and then join. So make sure you check this out, and join the BAAWC Rockstar Community!

Best Relationship Building Tool Ever!

In Chapter 9, I talked about sending a card to a list of media contacts with gift cards enclosed. This may sound like a lot of work, but it is actually very simple. I use a service called SendOutCards. This online service allows you to import and manage contacts, and send greeting cards (along with gifts and gift cards) using your computer. You select, create, and personalize each card (you can even add photos and videos), and they take care of the rest. That's right! They print, stuff, stamp, address, verify, and mail the card for you.

This has been a big time-saver for me, and the cards cost about a third of what you would normally pay. You can open and close your account at any time, and its only $9.80 per month to send up to 10 cards (you can do more of course). SendOutCards is on its way to becoming a multibillion dollar company and completely changing the way individuals and businesses send cards. It's similar to using Netflix rather than going to a movie rental store and paying $5 to rent a movie. More convenient, less expensive, and one of the best relationship building tools I have seen ever. Visit **www.sendoutcards.com/mattshoup** to see how this service works. I will even let you send a few free cards on me. Have fun!

More About Entrepreneur's Organization

In this book, I mentioned the impact EO has had on my life and entrepreneurial journey. This is a site that all BAAWC Rockstars must go check out: **www.eonetwork.org**. This site will explain what EO is all about and how you can become involved in their global network. As with most organizations like this, it does cost money. Let me tell you, the check I write to EO every year is worth every penny and more! Some of the biggest lessons I have learned have been a result of attending an EO event, retreat, or get-together.

EO consistently searches for the world's best speakers, coaches, and entrepreneurs to share their stories, ideas, and experiences with entrepreneurs all over the world. I could go on and on about the benefits, stories, and friendships I have created. Instead, just go check out the website, and get in touch with the chapter closest to you. To do this, from the home page, click on the Membership Application tab. On the page it takes you to, on the right side of the screen, click on "Find Your Chapter" to find the chapter closest to you.

Interviewees in This Book
If you would like to reach any of the people I interviewed in this book, please send an email to
ceointerviews@becomeanawardwinningcompany.com
and they will be forwarded to the interviewees.

• • • • •

Books I Love and Enthusiastically Endorse
I don't have a formal business degree and truthfully do not think such degrees give entrepreneurs any better chance of success. I have learned all my lessons from the school of hard knocks and getting out there and doing business, making mistakes, and improving myself. One of the ways that I am always learning, and growing is by reading. Leaders read, and readers learn and grow. I enthusiastically endorse the following books for all my BAAWC Rockstars, and consider each one a must-read.

The Bible
I love Jesus. You may, or you may not. Let me make a clear and accurate statement: the advice and values I offer in Chapter 20, Tips for the BAAWC Rockstar, are based on biblical principles. Whether you believe in the stories in the Bible as the truth of creation, God, Jesus, etc., many agree that if you run your business by biblical principles, you will win. Each one of the values I shared in Chapter 20 can be correlated to a story, verse, or lesson from the Bible. So go

pick one up if you don't have one. If you do, open it up
and think about how the content of the Bible applies to your
business.

Total Money Makeover by Dave Ramsey

I read this book and applied the concepts at a time in my life
and business when I was headed down a path of financial
destruction. Reading this book completely changed the
way I looked at and managed money. His points are simple,
systematized, and can be applied to anybody at any financial
point in their life or business.

EntreLeadership by Dave Ramsey

With his 20 years of business experience, he gives readers
advice on how to become an amazing entrepreneur/leader.

Onward: How Starbucks Fought for Its Life without Losing Its Soul by Howard Schultz

This book highlights the rise, near-fall, and turnaround of
Starbucks. It also gives us a look into who Howard Schultz
is as an entrepreneur, leader, and man who has plans to make
radical changes to better our country and world.

Start With Why by Simon Sinek

Simon's book talks about the importance of clarifying,
organizing, and sharing why you do what you do. This one
could very well be a game changer for you and your business.

The E-Myth by Michael Gerber

This book talks about how you can go from working in your

business to working on your business, showing how the technician can become the manager, step away, and grow.

Rockefeller Habits by **Verne Harnish**

The concepts and ideas in his book will leave you with a one-page strategic plan to grow your company. Very simple, concise, and to the point.

High Trust Selling by **Todd Duncan**

Knowing that all entrepreneurs need to learn sales, I think back to this book as the best, most inspiring, and memorable book I have read about sales. Todd delivers the right way to sell, and how to ask the right questions and build relationships that will last a lifetime. Plus, you will close a lot more business doing this. I almost doubled my close rate after I read this book.

Delivering Happiness by **Tony Hsieh**

The inspirational story of the Zappos company and brand, as well as the story of its leader and world-class entrepreneur, Tony Hsieh. All entrepreneurs should be applying the stories and ideas in this book to their business and life.

Toilet Paper Entrepreneur by **Mike Michalowicz**

This book breaks all the rules of the traditional academic book, and at the same time provides valuable information that every entrepreneur needs to know. Sit back and enjoy this one. You will be not only educated, but thoroughly entertained!

The Pumpkin Plan by **Mike Michalowicz**

If you enjoyed Mike's first book, you'll love the second book where he equates growing a giant world-class pumpkin with growing a giant world-class business.

The Sleeping Giant: The Awakening of the Self-Employed Entrepreneur by Ken McElroy

These 20 stories of successful entrepreneurs left me inspired, and will do the same for you.

MATT SHOUP, AUTHOR

29996241R00111

Made in the USA
San Bernardino, CA
04 February 2016